No More Reading Instruction Without Differentiation

DEAR READERS,

Much like the diet phenomenon *Eat This, Not That*, this series aims to replace some existing practices with approaches that are more effective—healthier, if you will—for our students. We hope to draw attention to practices that have little support in research or professional wisdom and offer alternatives that have greater support. Each text is collaboratively written by authors representing research and practice. Section 1 offers a practitioner's perspective on a practice in need of replacing and helps us understand the challenges, temptations, and misunderstandings that have led us to this ineffective approach. Section 2 provides a researcher's perspective on the lack of research to support the ineffective practice(s) and reviews research supporting better approaches. In Section 3, the author representing a practitioner's perspective gives detailed descriptions of how to implement these better practices. By the end of each book, you will understand both what not to do, and what to do, to improve student learning.

It takes courage to question one's own practice—to shift away from what you may have seen throughout your years in education and toward something new that you may have seen few if any colleagues use. We applaud you for demonstrating that courage and wish you the very best in your journey from this to that.

Best wishes,

— *Ellin Oliver Keene and Nell K. Duke, series editors*

No More Reading Instruction Without Differentiation

LYNN GERONEMUS BIGELMAN

DEBRA S. PETERSON

HEINEMANN
Portsmouth, NH

Heinemann
361 Hanover Street
Portsmouth, NH 03801–3912
www.heinemann.com

Offices and agents throughout the world

The authors and publisher wish to thank those who have generously given permission to reprint borrowed material:

Figure 3–3: Engagement Inventory from *Teaching Reading in Small Groups* by Jennifer Serravallo. Copyright © 2010 by Jennifer Serravallo. Published by Heinemann, Portsmouth, NH. All rights reserved.

Acknowledgments for borrowed material continue on page xii.

Library of Congress Cataloging-in-Publication Data
Names: Bigelman, Lynn Geronemus, author. | Peterson, Debra S., author.
Title: No more reading instruction without differentiation / Lynn Geronemus
    Bigelman and Debra S. Peterson.
Description: Portsmouth, NH : Heinemann, [2016] | Series: Not this, but that
    | Includes bibliographical references.
Identifiers: LCCN 2016010143 | ISBN 9780325074351
Subjects: LCSH: Reading (Elementary). | Individualized instruction.
Classification: LCC LB1573 .B47 2016 | DDC 372.4—dc23

LC record available at https://lccn.loc.gov/2016010143

Series editors: Ellin Oliver Keene *and* Nell K. Duke
Editor: Margaret LaRaia
Production: Vicki Kasabian
Interior design: Suzanne Heiser
Cover design: Lisa A. Fowler
Cover photograph: Christopher Futcher/Getty Images/HIP
Typesetter: Valerie Levy, Drawing Board Studios
Manufacturing: Veronica Bennett

Printed in the United States of America on acid-free paper
20   19   18   17   16   VP   1   2   3   4   5

To my father, Alfred Geronemus, my first teacher. He led a readerly life and passed on his love of reading to me.

To my mother, Terry Geronemus, for her love and encouragement.

To my children, Jeff, Jill, Ramin, Joey, Sharone, Jessica, and Scott, for the joy and pride they have brought me.

To my grandchildren, Jonah, Noah, Ethan, Ari, Jacob, Amelia, and Leah, who continue to delight me.

To my brother, Roy, and sister-in-law, Gail, for their unwavering support.

To Michelle Harris, Nell Duke, Ellin Keene, and Margaret LaRaia for believing in this work.

To my amazing Grayson staff and my colleagues in Waterford whom I continue to learn from daily.

My admiration and appreciation.

Lynn Geronemus Bigelman

I am so thankful for the support of my family: Mom, Dad, John, Laura, Rob, and Wally the dog. I feel very blessed to live each day in your love and encouragement.

Debra S. Peterson

CONTENTS

Introduction Ellin Oliver Keene   ix

SECTION 1   **NOT THIS**
One Size Fits Some
Lynn Geronemus Bigelman

When One Size Doesn't Fit Everyone   2

Planning Informed by Standards and Students   3

Differentiation *Is* Doable   6

SECTION 2   **WHY NOT? WHAT WORKS?**
All Students Need Differentiated
Reading Instruction
Debra S. Peterson

Effective Teachers Differentiate Instruction   9

Effective Differentiated Instruction Focuses on Important Knowledge and Skills   11

- *Rigor, Motivation, and Engagement*   13

Observation and Assessment Should Inform Differentiation   16

Grouping Patterns Affect Learning   19

- *Effective Practices for Differentiating Whole-Class Instruction*   23

- *Effective Practices for Differentiating Small-Group Instruction*   24

- *Effective Practices for Differentiating Independent Work*   25

Evaluating Your Instruction for Differentiation   29

Section 3 **BUT THAT**

30

Differentiated Reading Instruction in Your Classroom

Lynn Geronemus Bigelman

How Observation and Formative Assessment Inform Differentiation   31

- *Learning Targets and Performance Tasks*   32

- *Pretesting to Plan Whole-Class, Small-Group, and Individual Instruction*   36

- *Observing Student Engagement*   37

- *Student Self-Assessment*   39

- *Assessing and Deepening Student Understanding Through Talk*   41

Reading Workshop: A Daily Structure for Differentiation   43

Planning Project-Based Learning   47

When and How to Use Whole-Group Instruction   51

When and How to Use Small-Group Instruction   53

When and How to Use Independent Work Time   57

- *Conferring*   59

- *Setting Individual Learning Goals*   62

- *Planning Intervention*   63

Supporting Growth Beyond Our Expectations   64

Afterword Nell K. Duke   67

Appendix A: Formative Assessment Options   69

Appendix B: Project-Based Unit-Planning Template   73

References   77

INTRODUCTION

ELLIN OLIVER KEENE

I took a walk with a friend, Betsy, recently, and we talked about her experiences as a young reader. Her teachers realized that she was reading well ahead of the rest of her class and promised her mother, also a teacher, that they were going to "individualize" her reading instruction. What followed for Betsy was a program in which she was asked to read a series of comprehension passages on cards, answer the questions, and, if she got the answers right, she "got" to work on longer passages on different colored cards. Initially, she recalled that she was excited to be out of the endless round-robin reading that characterized her peers' reading "instruction," but it wasn't long before a paralyzing boredom set in, and she began to hide the books she loved in her desk, sneaking a moment to read whenever she could. It's a sad day in schools when a child has to sneak a moment to read a real book!

Educators have long chased the ideal of differentiated instruction, but our efforts, as Betsy recalled, haven't always been successful. The very idea of tailoring instruction for twenty-five children in one classroom seems overwhelming at best. As Lynn describes in Section 1 of *No More Reading Instruction Without Differentiation*, most of our attempts come from a deep sense of responsibility to meet students' very different needs, but they may come up short when we do things like ask everyone to read that favorite novel every year.

Without choice in what they read and the opportunity to work on authentic learning tasks—work that one might reasonably expect to do outside of an academic setting—we cannot truly differentiate for students. As Lynn reminds us, "we do have to ditch the decision making that leads us to teach in a sequence rather than according to student needs. When we don't plan according to the specific needs of the students in front of us, our instruction is all but guaranteed not to meet every student's needs."

In Section 2, Debra Peterson introduces us to the research on differentiating instruction and shows that, for at least the last forty years, we've understood that particular approaches to differentiation have made a significant difference in student achievement. As I read this section, I couldn't help but think of my friend Betsy's experiences as a young reader, and it becomes clear why she and many others didn't actually learn to become better readers through the "individualized" stairstep programs we've created over the years. Debra emphasizes that it is critical to engage students in higher-level thinking and to guide them to learning experiences that relate to their interests and have authentic audiences with whom they can share new knowledge and insights. The research is compelling and will provide readers with ample evidence to support more differentiated instruction in their schools and districts.

I wish that Betsy had attended a school like Lynn Bigelman's in the Detroit area. In Section 3, Lynn introduces us to teachers who would have supported Betsy as well as those who struggle to learn—and everyone else in between—in classrooms where project-based learning is the norm, where students have a great deal of choice in what they read and in how they share their thinking with others. In wonderfully practical detail, we get to see how teachers assess students' present performance and design subsequent learning experiences that are authentic and engage students in the higher-level thinking Debra calls for in Section 2. Readers will be able to see past the overwhelming idea of differentiation for each child to a new horizon in which children participate in their own assessment and designs for learning. She says, "In effective differentiated classrooms, students gather evidence of their own progress nearly as often as the teacher does. Even very young children can use a variety of means, in addition to talking and writing, to demonstrate their level of understanding in a way that reveals specifically what instructions they need next."

My friend Betsy ended up at Stanford Law School, is a successful environmental attorney, and is still a voracious reader. She was lucky to have parents who valued learning, read to her, and put books in her hands. I'm worried, however, about the children in classrooms right now who aren't privileged in the same way. Those kids need the approaches Lynn and Debra advocate in this incredibly useful book. You're about to be inspired to differentiate for the children in your life, and, as Lynn tells us, it's doable!

NOT THIS

One Size Fits Some

LYNN GERONEMUS BIGELMAN

As I wander through the department store searching for the perfect sweater, I am confronted by a multitude of styles, colors, textures, and sizes. In bold letters is a tag reading, "One size fits all." I know from firsthand experience that the tag should read, "One size fits some." People are amazingly diverse, and very little fits everyone.

This department store dilemma is not unlike the one present in every classroom in every town and city across our country. We cannot grab instruction from a shelf and assume it will fulfill the needs of all our students. Our decisions about what will work for each student must be informed by observation, assessment, and planning. Even though each year we strengthen our professional knowledge and plan our instruction, it is impossible to determine each child's needs until that child is sitting in front of us.

When One Size Doesn't Fit Everyone

As an educator, parent, and grandparent, I have witnessed what can happen when a child's needs are not met by one-size-fits-all instruction. In my second-grade classroom, high-spirited Kyle seemed to be making great leaps in reading. It looked to me as if he were comprehending, but he was reading texts only with pictorial support. When he began reading chapter books, I discovered he was missing some foundational skills. I realized this not because of any assessment I gave but because Kyle boldly asked me, "What is a /k/nife [pronouncing the k]?" He was struggling to decode words. My class instruction was focused on interpretation—specifically, themes in a text—but how could Kyle tell me what the ideas were if he couldn't read the words? This was an alarming awakening for me as his teacher.

Herein is revealed a significant obstacle in one-size-fits-all instruction. When we encounter a specific student's need, as I did with Kyle, we can adjust our instruction to meet that need, but we don't address the larger issue of other students' needs. It's like lengthening the sleeves of that one-size-fits-all sweater—it solves the problem for some, but not all, students.

> Just as a word may have different meanings in different contexts, so too do our instructional goals need to be contextualized for each student.

For example, when Angelous, an English language learner (ELL) student in my class, needed help understanding the word *table* in a text he was reading, I pointed to the table we were sitting at. We were both pleased with the clarity achieved. But later, during a whole-group lesson on multiplication tables, Angelous looked confused. He needed to understand that the word *table* had different meanings in different contexts. For ELLs, mistaken interpretations often stem from knowledge: The Spanish word *embarazada* means *pregnant*, whereas the English word *embarrass* means something quite different. Many words with similar Latin roots in English and Spanish have very different meanings. Without targeted, intentional observation, assessment, and planning, it is too easy to move forward with whole-group instruction and leave some students stuck in their confusion.

One-size-fits-all instruction doesn't work for all children because, obviously, children differ—in their knowledge and skills, in their interests, and in their cultural background. In elementary school, my son, regardless of the teacher or the text, was consistent in his disdain for reading. Also consistent was the fact that he was never given any choice in what he read. Several factors may have made a difference. For one, perhaps if he had been given more choice in selecting his reading material rather than being asked to read the same text all his classmates were reading, he may have discovered his love of reading much earlier. It was not until he was much older that he became an enthusiastic reader. Luckily, my grandson, a proud first grader, is being given some choice in his reading. His teacher has capitalized on his interest in informational texts about animals. He is now an excited and a highly engaged reader who can't wait to learn from books. This juxtaposition of generations reminds me that differentiated instruction, or the lack of it, has a lasting impact on students' lives.

Planning Informed by Standards and Students

Many of us mistakenly think we can meet a shared goal such as reading grade-level texts only by having all children read the same book. The same expectations for every student's learning do not mean the same instruction for every student. Unfortunately, the increased expectations delineated in the Common Core State Standards (CCSS) have caused many whole-group-only educators to feel defeated: They don't know how to support academically disenfranchised students. However, it's not the standards that are the enemy but the mode of instruction. Standards provide an opportunity to reconsider our instruction when we find our students challenged by the expectations.

Our standards do not define how we deliver instruction; instead, they define what we hope to accomplish by our instruction. However, because so many teachers have experienced only whole-class instruction, they cannot imagine another way. When words such as *differentiation* are used in education-centered conversations, many teachers shut down—they are not given enough support and/or clear models to be able to imagine doing this in their own classroom. In January 2015, James Delisle wrote a rebuttal to the practice of differentiation in *Education Week*, arguing that the difficulty of implementing differentiation makes it ineffective (www.edweek.org/ew/articles/2015/01/07 /differentiation-doesnt-work.html). Lack of models and support are two reasons teachers choose not to differentiate, but is the real reason difficulty of implementation or the inability to imagine what differentiation can look like? I argue it's the latter. In many schools and classrooms, teachers are being told they need to teach standards and differentiate their instruction so that all students can meet the expectations of these standards. But are they being shown how? Many see it as needing to provide individual lesson plans for each student, but that is not what is being suggested. As happens with students, when we hold teachers to an expectation they do not know how to meet, we risk creating resentment and disengagement. When we find ourselves feeling these emotions, we can re-center by focusing on the students in front of us.

> **Section 3 will show just how realistic (and rewarding) effective differentiation can be.**

> **Teachers can be prepared and differentiate; effective differentiation means planning and then adapting instruction based on individual students' needs, as you'll see in Section 3.**

When we assume we know our students' needs prior to seeing their shining faces or adopt a program that purports to meet all students' needs, our instruction is planned for imaginary children, not the ones in our classroom. Many teachers spend the summer planning their curriculum for the year, but a preplanned curriculum should not dictate our instruction to the exclusion of the students who enter our classroom at the end of August. Because we have only a year with our students, we must measure our learning in quantities of time, but sometimes this reality dictates our instruction more than the living, breathing students before us do.

When we aim for the whole class, what is our target? Is it what we think students at this grade level should know? Does this mean that on day fifty-nine of every school year we deliver a whole-class lesson on the theme in *Because of Winn-Dixie*, even if some students are struggling with basic comprehension and others already read the book last year?

We don't have to ditch our plans—based as they are on years of careful observation and reflection, they contain worthy resources. We do, however, have to ditch the decisions that lead us to teach according to a sequence rather than to meet our students' needs. When we don't plan according to the specific needs of the students in front of us in the moment, our instruction is guaranteed not to meet every student's needs. We set ourselves up to be ineffective. Too often, we don't address less-than-effective learning outcomes because we're afraid to question our own effectiveness as teachers, as if we cannot improve—we're either good teachers or we aren't, fixed and forever. As if our body, if good enough, should look perfect in the one-size-fits-all sweater. Great things happen when we allow ourselves to see that success or failure lies not in our fixed ability as educators but in our capacity to make wiser choices.

Let's extend this idea to that favorite novel we assign every year. Our passion for it is evident. Passion is contagious, right? But is this learning? The whole-class novel is a staple in many elementary classrooms. If we could step simultaneously into a large number of classrooms in which a whole-class novel is being taught, we would see the same things: every student seated at a desk, the novel in question in hand; little conversation among students; the teacher reading at the front of the room. Sounds like success, until you begin to look beneath the surface and notice a lack of engagement and relevancy, the boredom evident on many students' faces.

Despite the label, how can a "whole-class" novel serve the class as a whole? The readers sitting in the classroom have a variety of reading skills, experiences, and interests that remain unacknowledged. While the purpose of having every student read the same novel is to create community, we more often disengage the very students we are trying to inspire. Some students, skilled and passionate readers, experience impatience and resentment—why can't we recognize they want to read something different? Some students, struggling readers, experience low self-esteem because we are clearly communicating they should be able to understand the book—why can't we recognize they need to read something different? Many, even most, of the students don't feel seen by our instruction. Instead, they resent being given a size they've been told should fit them but doesn't. Instead of teaching them how to become better readers, we're teaching them how to pass time not learning. And we resign ourselves to fixed patterns of performance: Some students will struggle, and some students will do well.

Differentiation *Is* Doable

As the principal of an elementary school located thirty-eight miles northwest of Detroit in a diverse neighborhood where over 50 percent of our students are economically disadvantaged, I know what can happen when teachers are given the support they need to make differentiation happen in their classrooms. I also know what happens when they're not supported.

Differentiation means creating an instructional framework that allows choice and provides different scaffolds for meeting the same goals. It does not mean teachers need to invent scaffolds and choices or create lesson plans for each student. There is an abundance of research and exemplary practices we can use. We know

In Section 2, you'll learn the research that proves differentiation is worth arguing for.

Section 3 will show you how to make differentiated reading instruction work in your classroom.

that giving students choice invites and motivates them to be involved in their own learning. In this book, we argue for an instructional framework that asks teachers to adapt instruction based on the individual student's needs and interests. We show how to scaffold students' learning experiences toward lofty goals over the course of several months while also honoring children's uniqueness. I have seen many, many teachers find new joy in their profession, even after as many as twenty years of presenting traditional whole-class instruction, when they are encouraged to adopt differentiated instruction and given the support they need to do so. They experience firsthand how differentiating instruction can ignite or reignite the love of teaching and learning.

The research examined in the next section supports moving to a student-centered, authentic, academically rigorous learning environment for all children. The evidence is compelling: We must differentiate. Differentiated instructional practices not only promote student achievement and engagement but also are engaging to teachers. Research supports the integration of differentiation within our classrooms and begs us to replace old habits. Section 3 presents specific examples to help make differentiation happen in your classroom and school.

You're reading this book because you wonder whether there's another way. There is. Let us show you!

WHY NOT? WHAT WORKS?

All Students Need Differentiated Reading Instruction

DEBRA S. PETERSON

As Lynn explained in Section 1, one-size-fits-all instruction meets the needs of only some students. They vary in their knowledge, skills, cultural backgrounds, and interests so instruction needs to vary, too. Whole-class instruction has a place, but it will not provide the opportunities to differentiate that are needed. For example, if the whole class is asked to read the same book and respond in the same way, students who are reading above grade level may be bored or unchallenged. Students who are reading below grade level may be overwhelmed and frustrated. This does not lead to reading achievement for students in either group. Not surprisingly, observations of classroom instruction have shown that the longer students are in whole-group instruction, the more their time on task decreases (Taylor et al. 2003; Taylor and Peterson 2006). Disengagement does not facilitate learning (Guthrie et al. 2004; Pressley et al. 2007). Also, the more time students spend in whole-group instruction, the less time they spend on actually reading, writing, and talking about text (Taylor et al. 2003; Taylor and Peterson 2006).

Research has shown that when we don't address student diversity in the classroom, discrepancies in the learning opportunities provided to students of color and poverty and those who are English learners can occur (Hart and Risley 2003; NAEP Report 2014). This discrepancy, sometimes called "the achievement gap," refers to the persistent trend of lower test scores, graduation rates, and reading levels of some populations of students. "Closing the gap" is a major focus of education today, and studies of accomplished teachers have given us many examples of how differentiation can impact student learning.

Effective Teachers Differentiate Instruction

Many accomplished teachers are able to successfully meet the needs of all the diverse students in their classrooms. Multiple studies conducted in a variety of settings have identified and described what accomplished teachers were doing in their classrooms to positively impact their students' learning (see Figure 2–1). The studies listed below were not conducted in some perfect world with an elite population. Their findings were based on research in schools serving high percentages of students who were eligible for free and reduced-price lunch, students who were English learners, and students who were receiving special education services. Yet these schools were able to accelerate their students' achievement on standardized reading tests, demonstrating that they made more than a year's growth during a school year. This accelerated progress was evident for all students when results were disaggregated by gender, race, and achievement level. These studies have also shown that students were actively engaged in reading, writing, and talking about texts more than students in classrooms with less accomplished teachers. What were these teachers doing to foster this type of growth and engagement? Some of their promising instructional practices are summarized in Figure 2–1.

Figure 2–1 Instructional Practices of More and Less Accomplished Teachers

More Accomplished Teachers	Less Accomplished Teachers	Research
Frequently analyze student work samples and assessment data to inform daily instructional decisions and differentiate instruction	Less frequent use of student progress and performance data when determining what to teach	Foorman and Torgesen 2001; Graves, Gersten, and Haager 2004
Provide effective levels of whole-group and small-group instruction and independent work	Rely primarily on whole-group instruction	Allington and Johnston 2002; Pressley 2006
Provide different instruction and learning tasks for different students	Provide the same instruction and learning tasks for all students	Connors et al. 2011; Pressley et al. 2007
Establish rules and routines so that students can be self-regulated during independent work time	Instruction is more teacher-directed with little opportunity for student choice or autonomy	Bohn, Roehrig, and Pressley 2004
Engage students in more higher level thinking through talk and writing about text	Involve students in more lower-level thinking by asking more factual recall questions	Peterson and Taylor 2012
Provide challenging, rigorous, and motivating literacy activities	Provide lower-level, less rigorous activities	Pressley et al. 2003
Actively engage students in reading, writing, and talking about texts	Involve students in more passive activities like listening, watching, and taking turns reading or responding	Taylor et al. 2003

As you examine the list of instructional practices that were evident in the accomplished teachers' classrooms and compare them to other studies of effective reading instruction, you will note the overlap between what these teachers were doing and what research says works. This is not an accident! Teachers who are meeting the needs of all the students in their classrooms are implementing research-based practices on a daily basis. In the following sections, we will examine these practices in more detail.

Effective Differentiated Instruction Focuses on Important Knowledge and Skills

Research over the past forty years has shown repeatedly and consistently that a variety of factors contribute to students' growth and achievement in reading. These include school-level factors, curricular components, and instructional practices and strategies. A few of these critical components are summarized in Figure 2–2 to serve as an example of the complex nature of reading instruction.

As you can see from the examples listed here, many factors influence students' growth and achievement in reading. Just attending to the academic standards identified by the school district, state, or CCSS may not be enough to guarantee students' achievement. The academic standards provide guidelines for *what* should be taught at

> **For a process of breaking standards into daily goals for student learning**
>
> see Section 3, page 32

Figure 2–2 Examples of Factors Contributing to Students' Growth and Achievement in Reading

School-Level Factors	Curricular Components	Instructional Practices and Strategies	Research
Interventions provided to students needing more support in reading			Gunn et al. 2005; Mathes et al. 2005
		Motivating, engaging instruction incorporating student choice and collaboration	Guthrie et al. 2004

(continues)

All Students Need Differentiated Reading Instruction **11**

Figure 2–2 (*continued*)

School-Level Factors	Curricular Components	Instructional Practices and Strategies	Research
	1. Phonemic awareness 2. Phonics/word-recognition strategies 3. Fluency 4. Vocabulary 5. Comprehension		August and Shanahan 2006; Beck and McKeown 2007; Ehri et al. 2001; Graves, Gersten, and Haager 2004; Kuhn, Schwanenflugel, and Meisinger 2010; Kuhn and Stahl 2003; National Reading Panel Report 2000; RAND 2002

each grade-level, but they do not specify *how* the content and skills should be taught. Research presents evidence of instructional practices that are effective, but we also need to consider not only what works but for whom and under which conditions. While the traditional "labels" or groups of students that are commonly used in schools are problematic (e.g., not all English learners are the same), they do give us a structure to talk about the components of instruction that research has tested and proven to be more and less effective with students who fall into various categories of learners. These categories of learners will be used in the following sections for ease and simplicity of discussion but with the understanding that while students may have some characteristics in common, they will also vary greatly in their background knowledge, life experiences, oral vocabularies, and reading skills. That is one reason why differentiated instruction is so important. Accomplished teachers use the academic standards, their knowledge of research-based practices, and their understanding of individual students to provide instruction that is focused on the targeted skills and knowledge that various students need at a particular point in time. They also consider how they can match their instructional strategies to their students' specific knowledge, skills, cultural backgrounds, and interests.

Rigor, Motivation, and Engagement

Multiple studies have highlighted the importance of providing instruction that is appropriately rigorous, motivating, and engaging to students of all ages and skill levels (e.g., Guthrie et al. 2004; Pressley 2006; Taylor et al. 2003). These studies have identified some key characteristics of challenging and motivating instruction. Some of these include

- Higher-level talk and writing about text
- Student choice when selecting topics and materials
- Collaboration with peers
- Authenticity of tasks and audience
- Active responding (i.e., every student is reading, writing, talking with a partner, or manipulating materials) rather than passive responding (i.e., students are listening and taking turns reading, writing, speaking, or manipulating)

Higher-level thinking engages students in critical thinking about the texts they are reading. This is in contrast to lower-level thinking, which only requires students to recall factual information or give simplistic "right or wrong" answers to questions presented by the teacher. Higher-level thinking might include questions about the author's message or theme of a story, an analysis of characters' motivations during the story, and personal connections between the students' lives and the events or conflicts in the story. Higher-level thinking asks students to look for relevancy in the things they are reading and to intentionally make connections between the text and their personal experiences, cultural backgrounds, prior knowledge, and interests. Relevance for informational reading can also be stimulated by hands-on inquiry in the classroom and by building instruction on students' sense of wonder and curiosity about the world. Relevance has been shown to lead to increased motivation, engagement, and interest, as well as increased reading comprehension (Guthrie, McRae, and Klauda 2007).

When engaging students in higher-level thinking, teachers encourage or coach students to elaborate on their thinking and to say more about their conclusions. If students give brief responses like, "The character I like best is the kitty because the kitty is nice," the teacher might prompt the student to say more by asking, "What in the story made you think the kitty was nice? What did she say or do that was nice?" Students should also learn to ask their own higher-level questions. Their questions can be used for discussion during small guided-reading groups, can serve as writing prompts for independent writing, or can be used in student-led discussions (e.g., book clubs and literature circles).

Studies by Taylor and colleagues (Peterson and Taylor 2012; Taylor et al. 2002, 2003, 2005, 2007; Taylor and Peterson 2006) found that the more teachers engaged students in higher-level talk and writing about texts, the more growth and achievement they had on standardized reading tests. This was true for all students, including English learners and those receiving special education services. Other researchers have also identified the importance of providing students with opportunities to engage in higher-level thinking through writing and conversations with peers. Saunders and Goldenberg (1999) found that higher-level thinking was beneficial for English learners because peers helped each other access background knowledge, clarify word meanings, and develop an understanding of literary themes. Garas-York, Shanahan, and Almasi (2013), McIntyre and Moore (2006), and Teale and Gambrell (2007) have documented the positive impact of critical thinking for students from economically disadvantaged families. Guthrie and colleagues (2009) found that higher-level talk and writing about text within the Concept-Oriented Reading Instruction (CORI) framework had positive effects for both low- and high-achieving students.

Teachers can engage students in higher-level thinking when using a variety of materials including narrative, informational, print-based, and digital texts; grade-level content, and real-world artifacts (i.e., menus, brochures, bus schedules). Students should have many opportunities to select their own materials and topics based on their personal interests. They also benefit from engaging in purposeful and authentic tasks. Purcell-Gates, Duke, and Martineau (2007) found that when students have the chance to read and write for a real audience in a way that reflects real-world literate behaviors, they demonstrate increased knowledge about the purposes and features of the genre. For example, conducting a research report on an animal for a presentation given in class is less authentic than researching an animal to create a pamphlet that will be available for patrons of the local zoo. Writing a persuasive letter that is submitted to the teacher for a grade is less authentic than going to the school board meeting to present your argument for increased funding for a new playground. Instruction that is based on students' interests and provides authentic purposes and audiences can be accomplished through the integration of reading, writing, and the content areas. Integrated units of study allow for student inquiry and collaborative learning (Guthrie et al. 2004; Roehrig et al. 2013), which is motivating and engaging for students of all ages. Teachers might permit students to self-select their inquiry groups or may intentionally place students in small groups to facilitate the use of students' home languages (e.g., forming a group of native Spanish speakers and encouraging them to discuss their experiment in Spanish).

Lynn will provide many specific examples of how teachers do this in Section 3, but two such methods are the aforementioned Concept-Oriented Reading Instruction and project-based learning. Guthrie and his colleagues (2004) studied the effects of CORI where students have the opportunity to investigate and research science concepts as part of the reading curriculum. Hands-on experiences are provided to the students to stimulate interest, relevancy, and inquiry related to a big conceptual theme like "Plant and Animal Relationships." Students receive explicit instruction from the teacher but also have many opportunities to work cooperatively with their peers as they conduct and share their research. CORI has been shown to positively impact students' content knowledge and vocabulary, reading comprehension, motivation, and self-efficacy. When students are empowered, engaged, and motivated, they are more likely to persevere through complex texts and tasks (Guthrie, McRae, and Klauda 2007; Guthrie et al. 2009).

Project-based learning is another way to increase student engagement and motivation and to integrate content area topics and materials into literacy instruction (Halvorsen et al. 2014). Project-based learning incorporates components of inquiry (Barron and Darling-Hammond 2008; Lee et al. 2006), cooperative learning (Johnson and Johnson 2009), and problem-based learning (Wieseman and Cadwell 2005). When students are engaged in answering important questions about their lives and the world, when they have choices about the research and study they will do related to authentic questions, and when they have multiple opportunities to collaborate with their peers while the teacher coaches and gives feedback, then several positive results have been documented. For example, students' attitudes toward the content areas improved (Wiesman and Cadwell 2005), their knowledge and understanding of subject-area content is increased (Lee et al. 2006), and the achievement gap between students from differing socioeconomic backgrounds can be negated (Halvorsen et al. 2014). Engaging students in well-structured, project-based learning gives students the chance to use their language skills to explain, question, argue, critically analyze, and persuade. They can read and write about their topic using a multitude of genres including real-world artifacts (i.e., blogs, petitions, letters to the editor, advertisements, campaign posters) for authentic purposes and audiences.

Observation and Assessment Should Inform Differentiation

To match instruction to students' strengths and needs requires ongoing inquiry, observation, and data collection. This does *not* mean that we do more testing. It means that teachers and students are engaged in the daily process of gathering, documenting, and analyzing student work. When formative assessment becomes a part of instruction, it can provide meaningful evidence of student growth and learning and can inform the instructional decisions made about reading instruction. In studies by Heritage and her colleagues (2009, 2013), they describe the major steps of the process as

1. Providing students with clear, explicit learning goals and criteria of successful progress. For example, if the goal is to learn to write summaries of informational texts, then a rubric describing the components of quality summaries should be shared with the students before they complete the task. Anchor papers may also be provided so students can compare their work to other examples.
2. Gathering and interpreting evidence. Evidence includes progress-monitoring data, student work samples collected over time, anecdotal notes from a conference with an individual student, video recordings of student presentations, and so on.
3. Responding with modifications or adaptations to instruction. This might mean that the next day's instruction is adjusted so that the teacher can work with individuals or small groups to provide opportunities for additional coaching, conferencing, and guided practice. For the students who can already independently apply the targeted skills or content, additional challenge with more complex texts and tasks will be required.
4. Equipping students to set their own goals and to self-regulate their progress. Students can learn to document and record their own progress and to engage in self-evaluation using checklists, rubrics, anchor charts, and peer feedback.

Evidence should be authentic and multidimensional and should identify students' strengths as well as their needs. Examples of evidence might include students' written responses in reading journals, running records of oral reading, students' reading logs, rubric scores, portfolios of student work, or self-reflections on participation in a book club discussion. Students should be actively involved in this process and can record their progress in a variety of ways (i.e., graphs, checklists, portfolios, reading logs, audio and video recordings, exit slips).

The teacher can then use this information to decide on the types of reading materials and tasks that the students should encounter in the next days' lessons. For example, if in their summaries several students struggle to describe the author's purpose, the teacher may decide to model how to identify the big theme idea or author's message from a text. Snow, Burns, and Griffin (1998) stated that high-quality classroom instruction, instruction that is differentiated based on students' formative assessment data and prior performance, is the single-best defense against reading failure.

Matsumura, Patthey-Chavez, Valdes, and Garner (2002) identify the importance of formative assessment in providing specific teacher feedback to students about their progress. Specific feedback helps students know what they need to do to improve their own learning (Hattie and Timperley 2007). Discussing actual examples from ongoing student work makes the learning process very concrete to students and gives them the direction they need to make changes in their reading, writing, and speaking. Conducting individual or small-group conferences with students is one effective way to provide specific, targeted feedback on student work followed by opportunities for guided practice in the application of a highlighted skill or strategy (Glasswell 2001; McCarthy 1994). While little research on the effectiveness of different conferring practices currently exists, there is a wealth of research on the importance of providing specific, timely, and actionable feedback to students (Hattie 2009).

Teachers do not have to do this type of assessment and analysis of student work in isolation. Working as grade-level teams (including the specialists who work with those students), in content-area disciplines, with cross-grade professional learning communities, or with another trusted peer or literacy coach can make the process even stronger. Schools that regularly hold data retreats or data meetings can look at formative assessment data and student work samples to determine the effectiveness of schoolwide interventions, connect trends in student progress to professional development for the staff, and highlight the successes of grade levels and specific populations of students (Little et al. 2003; Peterson 2013b). Changes or refinements can then be made at the school, grade, or classroom level as teachers work together to provide consistent, cohesive, and differentiated instruction across the reading program.

Grouping Patterns Affect Learning

Many research studies have identified the effective use of whole-group, small-group, and independent activities as a key factor in effective reading instruction (Foorman and Torgesen 2001; Graves, Gersten, and Haager 2004; Taylor et al. 2000, 2003, 2005). Whole-group instruction should be kept short (i.e., approximately fifteen to thirty minutes depending on the age and developmental level of the students) and be used for teacher demonstration or modeling of skills

> **For guidelines on how to make various grouping structures work**
>
> see Section 3, pages 35–36

and strategies that will be beneficial to all students. Often this occurs through a teacher read-aloud or shared reading experience. Whole-group instruction can also be the time when teachers expose students to grade-level materials and content. The skills, strategies, vocabulary, and content modeled by the teacher in the whole-group situation should then be applied to the small-group instruction where the teacher can provide the guided practice and coaching that students need to be able to use their new learning.

Research provides an important caution for consideration when reflecting on the effectiveness of whole-group instruction. It states that high levels of time spent in whole-group instruction are negatively related to students' growth in reading (Taylor et al. 2005; Taylor and Peterson 2006). How does a teacher know if he or she is spending too much time in whole-group instruction? Indicators that the whole-group lesson is too long might include inattentive students, disruptive behaviors, loss of focus on the content or concepts being presented, nonresponsive behavior from the group, and difficulty applying the targeted skill or content to independent reading, writing, or speaking. Often when we are teaching, we are unaware of how long an activity or lesson is taking. Asking a trusted peer such as a literacy coach to observe instruction and record the amount of time spent on each section of the lesson may be informative and helpful when reflecting on the effectiveness of whole-group instruction.

Effective instruction also includes the use of small-group instruction each day (Taylor et al. 2000). This is the time when the teacher can support students as they apply new skills and strategies while actively reading and writing. This gradual release of responsibility (Pearson and Gallagher 1983) can occur when the teacher is there to coach and give feedback to individual students. Teachers can differentiate the amount of support they provide based on the skills and needs of the students in the small group. Students experience more success with new strategies and have greater access to the guidance of the teacher when in small-group instruction (Allington and Johnston 2002; Connor et al. 2011; Pressley 2006).

It is important to note that just placing students in small groups does not mean that the instruction is effective or differentiated. For example, if a teacher placed students in small groups and had each group rotate through multiple stations where every group did the exact same tasks using the exact same texts, then the small groups would not be differentiated. Or if the small-group instruction is based on students' instructional reading levels but does not address the individual differences in students' oral vocabularies, application of word-recognition strategies, background knowledge, or other factors that could impact learning, then the instruction will not be as effective. It is what the teacher does during the small-group time that makes the difference for student achievement. When the teacher's instructional decisions are informed by her knowledge of research, academic standards, formative assessment results, and understanding of the individual students, then effective differentiation can occur. Connor and colleagues (2011) found that when teachers varied their instructional focus for small-group instruction based on students' strengths and needs, students made more progress in reading. This finding is further supported by the research examining effective instruction for targeted groups of learners as discussed later.

Researchers looking at what works for students who are English learners have found that differentiation through small-group instruction is especially important because EL students demonstrate a wide range of oral language and reading skills (August and Shanahan 2006). This means they require a range of instructional supports that are difficult to provide when relying primarily on whole-group instruction. Small-group instruction allows the teacher to focus on the targeted skills that the students need to move them forward and to differentiate the groups based on students' language and reading skills (Graves, Gersten, and Haager 2004; Lapp, Fisher, and Wolsey 2009). This is also the time when the teacher can explicitly and intentionally connect the school curriculum to students' prior knowledge, cultural and linguistic backgrounds, and previous learning (Au 2005; McIntyre and Turner 2013). Incorporating a rich array of visuals, artifacts, real-life objects, and graphic organizers can also be done during small-group instruction. The use of realia and other visuals has been shown to help build students' oral vocabularies and background knowledge (August and Shanahan 2006; Helman 2009).

Students who are receiving special education services and who are mainstreamed into the general education classroom also require additional supports during reading instruction. Research studies including students who were identified for special services because they struggled with reading or writing revealed that small-group instruction was an effective means to provide the targeted instruction that these students needed to be successful (Chorzempa and Graham 2006; Elbaum et al. 2000). Multitiered levels of support like Response to Intervention (Fuchs, Fuchs, and Vaughn 2008) emphasize the importance of differentiation during core reading instruction. A study by Scanlon and colleagues (2008) demonstrated that when adaptations were made during core instruction, or tier 1, the need for more intensive interventions (tiers 2 and 3) were reduced because fewer students needed to be referred for special services.

For a model of intervention planning in action

see Section 3, page 63

Students who are not receiving special education services but who are reading below grade level also benefit from small-group instruction (Barr and Dreeben 1991; Taylor et al. 2005; Tyner 2009). Their progress can be accelerated when they receive targeted instruction by the classroom teacher focused on their specific strengths and needs during core instruction (Hiebert and Taylor 1998; Mathes et al. 2005; Taylor et al. 2007). Additional small-group or individual reading interventions that are provided to these students should be supplemental to and aligned with the core instruction. This alignment can occur only through collegial conversations and the shared use of assessment data between the grade-level teachers and the specialists. For example, students who are English learners may need interventions designed to build English language skills as well as reading skills (Gunn et al. 2005; NCEE 2014; Vaughn et al. 2006). Students receiving special education services may require interventions that provide more explicit and intensive instruction on the application of skills and strategies to the reading of connected texts than that regularly evident in guided reading groups (Foorman and Torgesen 2001). Collaboration between the specialists and the grade-level teachers is especially important because the adaptations that the general education classroom teachers can make to instruction during the core reading program can reinforce the skills and strategies that the students are learning in their special education or English language interventions and vice versa. When this occurs students are more likely to apply or transfer their learning from the intervention to a broader context.

Schools are also accountable for the reading growth of their students who are already reading at or above grade level. Often when we think of differentiated instruction, we forget to consider the students who are currently meeting the grade-level benchmarks. Research has shown that differentiation can also benefit the students who are skilled readers (Guthrie et al. 2004, 2009; Pressley et al. 2007; Sotor et al. 2008; Taylor 2013; Tyner and Green 2005). They also need to be challenged and motivated to continue to apply their skills and strategies to ever-increasingly more rigorous texts and tasks. Again, this is difficult to do during whole-group instruction with minimal differentiation of content, texts, or tasks.

Effective Practices for Differentiating Whole-Class Instruction

Whole-class instruction does not have to look like this: All students sit quietly and look at the teacher as he or she explains concepts and imparts information! Whole-class instruction can include partner and small-group work, self-selected reading related to a big theme or concept, and project-based learning inspired by inquiry. Multiple research studies have documented the impact of working in pairs or small student-led groups during reading instruction. Fuchs, Fuchs, Mathes, and Simmons (1997) have found that elementary students can effectively support each other in the review and reinforcement of a variety of reading skills and strategies through their Peer-Assisted Learning Strategies (PALS) program. PALS is a whole-class routine where students work with partners on phonemic awareness and phonics skills, passage reading to increase fluency, and questioning to clarify and monitor comprehension. Students also learn to coach each other in the use of word recognition and comprehension strategies and to give one another feedback. Palincsar and Brown (1986) demonstrated the effectiveness of reciprocal teaching where students worked in groups of four to implement a routine of comprehension strategies as they discussed texts and clarified meanings. Using student-led discussion groups can also be an effective way to differentiate instruction during whole-class instruction and they have been proven to improve students' growth and achievement as readers. These include book clubs (Goatley, Brock, and Raphael 1995); instructional conversations (Saunders and Goldenberg 1999); collaborative reasoning (Chinn, Anderson, and Waggoner 2001); and literature circles (Daniels 2002). Components of effective student-led discussions include student choice in the selection of texts, topics, or themes; student control of the conversation through the use of roles and student-generated questions; and scaffolded support provided by the teacher. Student-led discussions of texts support students' ability to ask questions, interpret text, explain their thinking, and cite evidence from the text, all of which are important skills stressed in many states' academic standards including the Common Core State Standards. Student-led groups can increase students' motivation and engagement because they are actively engaged in reading, writing, and talking about texts with their peers (Peterson and Taylor 2012; Taylor et al. 2003). This is in direct contrast to the passive responding that occurs in most whole-group instruction where students spend most of their time listening and taking turns responding or reading.

Effective Practices for Differentiating Small-Group Instruction

Multiple studies by Taylor and colleagues (2000, 2002, 2003, 2005, 2006, 2007) document the need to differentiate instruction during small-group instruction. Even within a small group, students display a variety of knowledge, skills, cultural background, and interests. Teachers can accomplish differentiation by making some simple adaptations to instruction. For example, instead of having students take turns reading (i.e., round-robin reading, popcorn reading), they can ask students to chorally read, read with a partner, silently read, or whisper read (i.e., each student quietly reads aloud at his or her own pace so the teacher can listen in and coach as needed). These methods keep all students actively engaged in reading, which we know from research is positively related to students' growth and achievement (Peterson 2013a; Taylor et al. 2002, 2003). Instead of calling on one student at a time to ask or answer a question, the teacher could ask the students to turn to a partner and share their ideas or questions. The teacher can listen to the individual conversations and coach students to elaborate on their ideas as needed. Students could also write their questions or responses in journals, on whiteboards, or on digital devices. Again, these strategies provide opportunities for every student to think and formulate a response rather than just one or two students at a time. Providing opportunities for every student to read or answer questions may be more difficult or time consuming in classrooms where mainly whole-group instruction occurs, but for students who struggle with grade-level reading and content, waiting for a turn in the whole group can generate disinterest and disengagement. That is why active responding is so important to consider during both whole-class and small-group instruction.

Effective Practices for Differentiating Independent Work

When thinking about differentiated instruction, a common question is, "What are the rest of the students doing while I am working with a small group?" The answer is that students should be reading and writing! Research has shown that elementary students who read for thirty or more minutes a day in school have higher results on their standardized tests than students who read for less time (Miller and Moss 2013; Reutzel, Fawson, and Smith 2008). For kindergarten students, independent reading might include handling books, looking at pictures, rereading simple texts like song or poem charts, and listening to audio recordings of books. They might begin the school year by doing this for five minutes at two different times during the school day. As the year progresses, kindergarten teachers can gradually increase the time spent in independent reading and add in activities like partner reading, reading short readers' theater scripts, and rereading texts used in small group instruction. For students in grades one to six, independent reading activities might include:

- Rereading texts used in whole-class or small-group instruction
- Rereading class-created books
- Reading self-selected texts (i.e., magazines, chapter books, informational texts, digital texts)
- Reading with a partner
- Rehearsing a role from a play or a readers' theater script
- Conducting an author study by reading about the author on the author's website
- Researching a topic for a science or social studies unit

Students also need multiple opportunities to write and talk about what they have read (Garas-York, Shanahan, and Almasi 2013; Peterson and Taylor 2012). Writing in response to literature might include activities like the following:

- Answering teacher-generated higher-order questions (e.g., *Think of a time when you had a disagreement with a friend. What happened? How did you resolve your disagreement? Would you have handled it differently if you could do things over again? Why or why not?*)
- Writing student-generated higher-order questions to ask in small student-led discussion groups
- Creating class blogs or discussion forums with students around the world

- Creating real-world resources like pamphlets, brochures, informational booklets, websites, field guides, newsletters, and so on
- Writing book reviews and posting them online

Differentiating instruction does not mean that a teacher has to create individual learning plans for each student in the classroom—that would be an overwhelming and monumental task and would be difficult to maintain on a daily basis. Differentiation can be accomplished by varying the difficulty of the texts, tasks, or support that students require to successfully complete the task. Activities can also be structured so that students who require more challenge can accomplish more rigorous tasks. Differentiation can also be based on students' interests or cultural backgrounds. For example, the teacher might form small groups of students based on their cultural heritage and ask them to read and discuss a fable from their culture. At another time, he or she might form small groups that encompass multiple cultural perspectives to add depth and richness to the interpretation of the text.

Research on effective instruction provides some tips for structuring or managing independent work time that are important to consider when establishing a new or modified routine in the classroom (Bohn, Roehrig, and Pressley 2004; Tyner 2009; Tyner and Green 2005). A few are listed here and more examples will be provided in Section 3.

- Take time to establish routines. You may want to introduce one center or independent activity at a time while you are there to monitor and give feedback to the students.
- Model how to accomplish the independent work. Demonstrate the activity several times, and provide time for guided practice. Make sure students know what to do when they have questions about the work. Post anchor charts to remind students to use strategies when they encounter difficult or unfamiliar words or content.

- Build in accountability by developing "quality work rubrics" with the students. Provide checklists or other tools to help students monitor their own progress. Post examples or models of the finished product so students can self-evaluate the quality of their work.
- Provide opportunities for student choice by giving students a "menu" of options (e.g., writing and presenting a book talk, creating an audio-visual book trailer, developing a PowerPoint presentation).
- Provide opportunities for student collaboration. Teach students how to work with partners or small groups without adult guidance. Provide sentence stems that students can use when talking with their peers. Prompts like, "I was wondering about . . . ," "This part of the text reminded me of . . . ," or "I enjoyed this part of the text because . . ." can support students as they are moving toward student-led discussions.

Moving from teacher-directed, whole-group instruction to differentiated instruction that is more student-focused can be a daunting task to consider. To begin the move toward more differentiated instruction, there may need to be a change in the class schedule. Section 3 will present some examples of schedules that include an effective use of whole-class instruction, small guided-reading groups, pairs and student-led groups, and independent work.

Differentiated instruction allows students to work both in grade-level material and content (with appropriate support and scaffolding) and in texts that are matched to their individual knowledge, skills, cultural backgrounds, and interests. If students are exposed only to texts that are too difficult for them to read, they may become frustrated and give up. Students who experience this may exhibit avoidance behaviors that serve to reduce the amount of time they have to struggle through overwhelming tasks. Other students may find that the grade-level material is too easy, and they may become bored and off-task as a result. Differentiated instruction allows the teacher to present skills and strategies that are challenging for the entire group while providing time for the targeted skills-based instruction many students need to grow in their abilities as readers and writers.

Evaluating Your Instruction for Differentiation

As you reflect on the information and examples in this section, you may want to ask some questions about your instruction and the degree to which you are currently differentiating instruction for the specific students you serve. If you are an administrator or literacy coach, you may want to consider the reading instruction that is being delivered across your school or district. Figure 2–3 has a few questions to get you started in your reflection process. Perhaps as you reflect, you will celebrate the ways your school has worked to serve the needs of all students. Perhaps you will generate ideas for things that could be refined or added to what you are already doing. To aid you in that process, Section 3 will present some classroom examples and practical ideas from the amazing teachers in Lynn's school.

Figure 2–3   Questions for Reflection on Differentiated Instruction

1. To what extent am I providing an effective amount of time for students to work in whole-group, small-group, and independent activities? How might the schedule be adjusted to meet various students' needs?

2. How am I collecting and using formative assessment data to make instructional decisions that will support all the students in my classroom? What other information might I need?

3. To what extent am I building on students' background knowledge and prior learning during reading instruction? What else could be done?

4. To what extent am I engaging all students in higher-level thinking as they talk and write about text? How am I coaching students to elaborate and expand on their responses?

5. To what extent are the independent activities students are completing differentiated, challenging, rigorous, and motivating? What else could be done?

SECTION 3

BUT THAT

Differentiated Reading Instruction in Your Classroom

LYNN GERONEMUS BIGELMAN

In the previous section, Debra explained that the more time students spend in whole-class instruction, the less time they have to read, write, and speak. That's a compelling reason to differentiate our instruction, but how do we help each child learn according to her or his needs? Each child is different. Children may be the same age, in the same grade, but they come to us with a range of readiness levels, interests, and experiences. Our charge is to ensure ongoing learning by responding to their individual needs. Every child must have the opportunity to make continuous progress regardless of reading level, content knowledge, or English language proficiency.

As a principal, it's my responsibility to make sure this happens throughout my school in a way that also respects teachers—one that is realistic, adaptable, and worthy. This section provides models and guidelines that make differentiation possible. These examples are not exhaustive; they demonstrate possibility and suggest ways you can evaluate and revise some of your own favorite practices for differentiation.

Grade-level expectations are communicated by the CCSS, state standards, and school culture, but these expectations are only the goal. They do not tell us how to get there. An essential truth about differentiated instruction is that there are many paths to the same goal. The destination is grade-level content understanding, but what we do to get there—how fast we go, where we pause, the detours we take—is determined by the students in front of us. We look to specific students at one moment in time to help us decide which skills are most relevant, most needed by them, and what context can help engage them.

McKenzie is a first-grade teacher expected to teach the standard *identify the main topic and retell details of the text (informational)*. She knows this goal is important because it's a strategy student readers can use to ground themselves in what an informational text is saying. McKenzie wants her students to understand that when they're curious about a topic, they can use informational texts to teach themselves more about it. As she thinks this standard through, she realizes there is a great deal of knowledge hidden within it and lots of activity implied but not specified. What skills and understanding inform the standard? What does the student have to know or be able to do in order to meet the standard? And how do students know that what they're learning each day is helping them get smarter, better at reaching this important goal?

How Observation and Formative Assessment Inform Differentiation

Formative assessment keeps our instruction informed by standards but responsive to individual students' needs by helping us make wise decisions about instruction and practice for children with a wide range of performance levels and needs. As Debra noted in Section 2, formative assessment does not mean more testing. It includes *oral*, *written*, and *artistic* ways to share thinking and growth toward a goal (see Appendix A). Most formative assessments are quick evaluations

Identify the variety of students whose needs are not met by one-size-fits-all instruction and how differentiation can solve the achievement gap

see Section 2, pages 8–9

based on children's work samples, talk, and writing. Evidence should be authentic and multidimensional and focus on students' strengths as well as their needs, as you'll see in the examples that follow.

Learning Targets and Performance Tasks

The first step in assessment is to know our learning targets and the major performances we want students to be able to do. To make a learning standard accessible to all students, we give them language for the skills and content involved. Learning targets are short-term goals or statements about what students should know and be able to do after instruction. They break down the standard's goals into lesson-sized chunks of learning (Moss and Brookhart 2012). A learning target provides the shared language the teacher and students use to talk about learning collectively—this is what we are aiming for as a class together right now—and individually—this is what you've accomplished, this is what you can try to do next. Learning targets never exist in isolation; they're always partnered with specific performance tasks that ask students to show evidence of what they've learned.

When I walk into a classroom in my school, I know the teachers will have communicated the daily learning target and the performance tasks—the success criteria—that they and their students can use to evaluate that day's learning. I also know I'll see students working on differentiated versions of the target. For example, when I enter McKenzie's classroom and see the day's learning target—*identify the main topic and retell details of the text (informational)*—I see small groups working on varied skills related to the target. One group reads a paragraph about the homes of people indigenous to North America and highlights the main topic. The task is brief, because McKenzie will check on these students and give them another task based on how they did with this one. Another group reads an article on construction techniques and tools of indigenous people, then identifies key words. A third group reads a text about nomadic indigenous tribes and organizes the main idea and supporting details within alphaboxes (Hoyt 2008). McKenzie is differentiating her instruction based on her students' reading levels and understanding of the concept, but every student knows the day's work will bring him or her closer to meeting or exceeding the learning target, and all students are gathering important background knowledge related to indigenous people that they will use to create guided tour podcasts for the Michigan Heritage Museum. When students return to whole-group instruction, they'll contribute bits of knowledge that will build a collective understanding of home construction for nomadic and settled indigenous people, bringing everyone closer to the shared learning target.

Our students need to share our vision for their learning because it is *their* learning. Learning targets help students articulate individual goals. All students need to name learning targets and know these goals are attainable with our guidance and their hard work. Empowered learners set goals, create a plan to meet those goals, and monitor their progress. Even our youngest students can articulate their strengths in reading, writing, and content areas and what they need to do to improve. They proudly document their learning progress in their own data notebook, in which slope graphs, bar graphs, and pictographs track their progress (see Figure 3–1). Of course, learning targets and goals are not in and of themselves motivating for readers; it's when we situate these targets and goals within the authentic context of projects and experiences that demonstrate the purpose of their learning that we truly give children an opportunity and reason to grow. When we make their growth a tool of communication not just with them but with their family and (when appropriate) their peers, we celebrate their progress through their relationships. When children realize they are making progress and are part of a community that recognizes their progress, they become invested in continuing to grow.

Figure 3–1   Student Writes in Her Data Notebook

When some or all students have difficulty meeting a day's learning target, teachers know they must adapt their plan for the next day's instruction. The learning targets approach has been described as a GPS system—a personal navigational tool that guides learning in achievable bits, offers assistance along the way, and helps students get back on track when they have difficulty. Figure 3–2 shows how McKenzie translated this standard into specific learning targets and performance tasks that allowed her to assess those targets.

When my staff and I gather to evaluate our learning targets and performance tasks, it's not uncommon for us to discover that our instruction doesn't cover all the learning expected by the standards or the performance task and that we are assessing skills we haven't taught. That's why identifying lesson targets and performance tasks is essential to differentiation. If we don't translate standards into what we will

Figure 3–2 Turning a Standard into Student-Friendly Learning Targets and Performance Tasks

Standard	English Language Arts Standards, Reading: Informational Text, Grade1: *Identify the main topic and retell details of the text*
Learning Targets	• I can use informational texts to learn new information. • I can identify an informational text by purpose and sometimes by features (captions, photographs, headings) and purpose (to inform the reader about a topic). • I can identify the topics addressed in an informational text. • I can identify what topic the text is mostly about (main topic and purpose). • I can identify the important details about the main topic. • I can retell those details in logical order. • I can consider the purpose of organization in an informational text.
Performance Task	Student performs research, reading, and taking notes on a variety of sources, including Internet searches and personal interviews.

teach and expect children to be able to do, our teaching will automatically exclude students who don't already know the content or who can't teach themselves. Every teacher learns from doing this work and knows the work will improve their instruction. Fourth-grade teacher Nichole Rinehart says, "Learning targets help to take the question out of what the students will be learning and helps students ground themselves in the work they are doing."

The act of listing performance tasks generates endless possibilities for inspiring learning. For example, the performance task *perform research, reading, and taking notes on a variety of sources, including Internet searches and personal interviews* could be achieved by creating a pamphlet on the local ecology, a short film on a historical figure, or a class science magazine containing articles written by each student, among many other options. Effective differentiation offers space for teacher and student creativity. Teachers make choices about how to teach the required skills and content based on who their students are and what context will most help make the required skills and content relevant and purposeful. The students choose topic and form based on personal interest, increasing engagement, and deepening learning. Students who say, "School is boring" are telling us that they need to be invited to investigate a topic that interests them. Performance tasks define what we will teach children, but they don't limit what children may learn.

Pretesting to Plan Whole-Class, Small-Group, and Individual Instruction

Once we've planned a unit, we have to decide which knowledge, skills, and strategies to teach in whole-group instruction and which instruction needs to be directed to individuals and small groups. We need to know exactly where students are in their learning in order to support them to go further. A pretest is essential in gathering this data. No grades are attached; the pretest merely tells us how to tailor our instruction and let students know what they will be learning.

Ideally, a pretest should correlate closely with our list of identified learning targets. That way we can make strategic adjustments to our instructional plan. If we hand out someone else's pretest without careful consideration, we won't know how well the pretest measures what we are hoping to teach. Therefore, it's important to identify learning targets before we pretest.

Pretesting helps us launch the year by differentiating, even when we don't yet know our students well. We can use the pretesting data when forming our initial small groups, but they rarely stay together for long; we form, disband, and reform groups based on observed needs and current performance levels throughout the year.

Early each school year, Elissa assesses her first graders' present performance in reading using the Developmental Reading Assessment.

While reading with each student, she keeps track of fluency, number of self-corrections, and retelling skill. She determines reading rate and accuracy. She pays attention to whether the child uses one or more strategies to monitor and self-correct or just keeps reading when she or he miscues. She also notes whether the miscue makes sense. She notices which strategies a struggling reader uses when decoding unknown words and which letter-sound relationships and word types give the reader difficulty so she knows what to focus on during small-group word study. She identifies which explicit reading strategies and letter-sound relationships to teach each child. She has the child retell the story, paying close attention to language borrowed from the text, whether character names or pronouns are used, the amount of detail included, event sequence, and how many times the student needs to be prompted for more information. She uses this information to create reading groups based on specific skill and strategy needs. These groups are fluid and change as Elissa gets more specific insight into each child's needs through observation and formative assessment.

Teaching is part research, and we often uncover new understanding about content and how students learn it as we present our instruction. A pretest may sometimes show gaps we did not expect in students' ability to achieve our learning targets. When these gaps are present in just a few students, we can present appropriate small-group and individual instruction. For example, after administering a pretest on personal narrative, Marissa, a fifth-grade teacher, discovered that Jason's word choice was extremely restricted; he used mostly single-syllable words. So, she included individual work with Jason on vocabulary acquisition in her word study instruction.

Observing Student Engagement

Once students begin practicing the skills we are teaching, we can assess their learning by observing their engagement. (This also lets our students know their work matters.) Given the flurry of classroom activity, it can be difficult to stand back and observe. But just three or four minutes of uninterrupted observation of children at work provides so much insight into their engagement and specific learning needs. Who is sharpening her pencil for the third time? Who is visiting the classroom library for the third time in as many days and starting yet another new book? Who is fake-reading? Which buddy readers are working together effectively? Who is completely engrossed in his book? Who needs immediate assistance? Imagine what it tells us about a child when we observe her explain to another child how a jellyfish is able to sting. This depth of knowledge is far greater than her reading level suggests. She is bringing something rich to the reading, a richness we need to tap into if she is to grow as a reader.

Observations are especially valuable if we resist the temptation to intervene immediately when we see a problem, withhold comment, and watch how students go about solving it. Or we can point out role models. If third grader Liza is slow getting down to work, we can ask her to observe other students jumping right into their independent reading and writing. Many teachers find it eye-opening to use an engagement inventory like the one in Figure 3–3.

Another way to differentiate based on observation is to share problems we notice with the individual or small groups involved and discuss the issue: getting to work in a timely way, for example, or selecting books children are willing to stick with. When Chase's teacher Nichole notices that he spends more time looking out the window and at her than reading his book, they have an on-the-spot reading conference. He says his book is boring, so she asks him to tell her about something, anything, he has found interesting recently. Chase mentions a TV mystery he watched the night before, so Nichole suggests an action-packed mystery from the classroom library and says if he doesn't like that, she'll have more options for him tomorrow. With the help of our school librarian, a plethora of mysteries appear in Nichole's classroom library the next day. In another classroom Megan observes three children constantly socializing rather than reading quietly, she forms a three-member book club, so they have a reason to talk grounded in text.

Figure 3–3 Engagement Inventory

Teacher: _____

Observation of: Reading   Writing   Both

Date: _____

Times Student Names									

Key: ✓ or blank = reading or writing   O = other off-task behavior

  SS = student-to-student talk about text   R = reacting to text

  W = looking out window   T = looking at me (*teacher*)

(Serravallo 2010, 22)

I encourage my teachers to seize the opportunity, even if just for a moment, to watch children working (or not working) and think carefully about how they can help them solve problems independently and set individual goals.

Student Self-Assessment

In effective differentiated classrooms, students gather evidence of their own progress nearly as often as the teacher does. Even very young children can use a variety of means in addition to talking and writing to demonstrate their level of understanding in a way that reveals specifically what instructions they need next. Every student should be empowered to reflect on where she or he is at a specific learning moment: "Do *I* understand? *How* do I know I understand? *What* do I think I need to understand?" Students know that not understanding something doesn't define them as failures; rather, it tells them and their teacher what they need to do next. This is a crucial step to teaching all students to become self-advocating learners.

Student self-assessment can be simple, as low-risk as a quick gesture or a private note (an "exit ticket") handed to the teacher following instruction. The fist-to-five strategy (see Figure 3–4) allows us to gauge quickly whether students are confused or clear about a whole-class lesson, but it's not perfect. The gesture communicates *students'* perception of their understanding, not necessarily its depth or accuracy. Nevertheless, self-assessment is an important habit that helps students pay attention to their learning, so they can then communicate what they need to their teacher or, ideally, differentiate their learning themselves.

There's no one best way to accomplish these quick check-ins, additional examples of which are listed in Figure 3–5. The important thing is to make sure it's done throughout instruction, particularly in whole-group settings. (We'll discuss frequency when we talk about classroom structures to support differentiation.)

Figure 3–4   Fist-to-Five Self-Assessment Chart

Figure 3–5 Additional Forms of Quick Student Self-Assessment

- *Thumbs*. Children indicate thumbs up if they understand the learning target, thumbs sideways if they have some understanding (*I almost get it*), or thumbs down if they have no understanding (*I'm lost*).

- *Response boards*. Students write a quick response on individual whiteboards to indicate the extent of their learning.

- *Exit tickets*. Children respond to a question on a small piece of paper, index card, or sticky note and turn it in on the way out of the classroom. Their responses are used to plan future instruction.

- *Reading-response sticky note icons*. Children use icons on sticky notes (see the examples in Figure 3–15) to indicate their responses to their reading.

Assessing and Deepening Student Understanding Through Talk

About talk being essential in promoting higher-level thinking skills

see Section 2, page 14

Perhaps the best way to demonstrate and simultaneously deepen understanding is through talk. Researcher Douglas Barnes (1976) has said, "Learning floats on a sea of talk." Conversation of this kind is an essential opportunity for formative assessment *and* differentiated instruction. A student explains his or her thinking, which invites questions and responses from other students and from us, deepening and broadening both individual and collective understanding. It's not the staccato interchange of a question-and-answer session but a more engaged back and forth, in which we as teachers, as well as other students, can elaborate or clarify in the moment. Think about it as expansive assessment: Here's what I (the reader) know, and here's how I'll grow through this conversation.

Not all students are comfortable with this kind of talk—they may not have yet experienced it in school; it might not be valued outside school; they may be acquiring English and are hampered by limited vocabulary and unfamiliarity with English syntax; they may be introverted; or they may not want to engage fully right then for a variety of reasons (a bad day, and so on). These are all fair reasons for hesitation, and our job is not to make students feel unsafe. Part of differentiation is recognizing the just-right challenge for individual students. We don't force all conversations into a whole-class discussion nor force every student to contribute. Instead, we look for talk opportunities throughout the day, in small groups and conferences and as a class. The sentence scaffolds in Figure 3–6 are a valuable tool for encouraging reticent students to talk and can be used to introduce all students to a variety of conversational strategies.

Figure 3–6   Sentence Scaffolds for Talk

Say Anything	Say Something Relevant	Say Something Back
Say something out loud in response: • I like . . . • I have . . . • Once I saw . . .	Say something connected to the conversation: • I noticed . . . • I think . . . • I wonder . . . • This reminds me of . . .	Respond to what someone else said: • I agree with . . . because . . . • I disagree with . . . because . . . • I can add on to . . . • My thinking is like yours because . . .
Say Something to Request Clarification	**Say Something to Revise or Improve**	**Say Something to Provoke or Extend**
If you are confused, say so and explain why: • Can you say more about that? • Could you say that again? • I think that because . . . • What do you mean by . . . ? • Can you tell me why you think that? • Can you explain that to me another way?	If you agree or disagree with something someone else said, it's okay to say so: • At first I was thinking . . . , but now I'm thinking . . . • I think the author is trying to say. . .	Say something that will continue the conversation or that others can respond to: • I started to change my thinking when . . . • I see what you're saying, but what about . . . • The surprising thing about this is . . . • This is important to notice because . . .

Waterford School District

These discussion techniques invite all students, regardless of ability, to contribute to class discussions. When they talk about their learning, they own their learning. Some students are good talkers who cover a lack of essential skills. Fifth grader Jack kept his class entertained with his amusing digressions but avoided the discussion topic. Making him aware of some add-on strategies helped him keep his conversation focused. Now that there are fewer digressions (entertaining though they be), Jack is able to practice his learning skills, and his teacher has a more specific sense of what he knows and is able to do.

Reading Workshop: A Daily Structure for Differentiation

All forms of observation and assessment work best when they are embedded in a recurrent structure, one that we and students can anticipate as part of our daily teaching and learning. We can't know whether students have mastered a learning target without giving them opportunities to practice and respond to assessment. To learn, students need time to try and fail without consequences. They need a structured time and place in which they come to own the learning targets as habits. As Annie Dillard (2013) says, "A schedule defends from chaos and whim. It is a net for catching days. It is a scaffolding on which a worker can stand and labor with both hands at sections of time."

Recurrent structures of time and space scaffold learning and teaching. Structure instills habits that help children outgrow themselves. When students have the predictability of a daily reading workshop, they know they will have the opportunity to practice and get the support they need. This structure also allows us to differentiate our instruction for every student.

In the workshop approach to literacy instruction (see Figure 3–7), we provide whole-group instruction in a minilesson. We clearly display and reiterate the learning target so that students are able to articulate their goal for the day. Then, as the students independently apply what they learned during the minilesson and discover what's

Figure 3–7 Workshop Structure

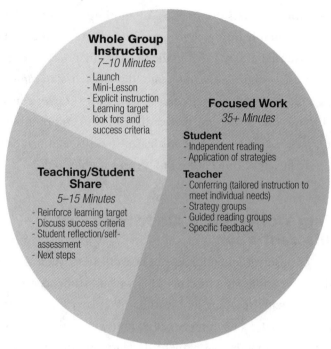

difficult and what's exciting for them, we work with small groups of children we've assembled based on assessment as well as confer with individual students. This small-group instruction includes intervention, extension, and conferences. Figure 3–8 delineates how this plays out in the classroom.

Each of the differentiation opportunities in Figure 3–8 provides opportunities to respond to students' needs. For example, when Sarah presented this lesson, she noticed that Angelous was struggling with the word *embarrass*, because a similar-sounding word means *pregnant* in Spanish. Sarah explained to Angelous and his partner that there are several English words that sound like Spanish words with different meanings and clarified the meaning of the English word *embarrass*. Later, she worked with a small group comprising Angelous and two other native Spanish speakers, using illustrations, music, movement, and synonyms and antonyms to clarify the differences between the meaning of some other Spanish words and similar-sounding English words.

Figure 3–8 A Sample Reading Workshop Minilesson

	Lesson 3
Teaching Point	Readers can determine importance in an informational text to summarize information.
Learning Target	I can write an informational text summary using the important ideas from the text.
Materials	

- Reading folders
- "Facing Your Fears" (article about . . .), printed copies and displayed on SMART board
- Summary planners
- List of steps
- Partnership assignments
- Interview with the author

Connection	"We have been working on reading and understanding informational text. We have worked on finding main ideas and key supporting details. Yesterday we worked on stretching our jottings into complete sentences. Today I want to teach you how we will write an informational text summary using our important ideas. Summarizing helps a reader think about what the most important information in a text is. We'll use our summaries to help Mrs. Kubiak's class identify which articles they might want to use for their research projects."
Demonstration/ Teaching	• Display the article "Facing Your Fears" on the SMART board. • Go over the complete sentences written yesterday. • Show the first sentence in the summary.
Guided Practice	• "Turn and talk with your partners about what you would add to our summary." • "Share what you came up with." • Write the complete sentences on the SMART board. • Allow students to take notes.

Figure 3–8 (*continued*)

	Lesson 3
Recap	"Today we started writing a summary of 'Facing Your Fears.' As you claim your reading spot today, I want you to continue to capture your thinking on sticky notes as you read independently today. Focus your notes on the most important ideas you might include in a summary. When you are done, please read your independent reading book. Are there any questions?"
Focused Work Time	• Conduct partnership and individual conferences to make sure students are rereading their piece and focusing on the second section. • Have students write their summaries on the summary planner. • Support partnerships as they work. • Take anecdotal notes using your preferred note-taking system. • During this time, the teacher is likely working with a needs-based small group.
Sharing	• Gather students back on the carpet for a sharing session. • Ask students to have their summary planners in front of them and be prepared to share their summaries. • Ask a few students to share.
Lesson Closure	• "Show me on a fist of five [see Figure 3.6] how you would assess your progress as a summary writer of nonfiction."
Lesson Extension	• After students have provided self-assessment and you've conferred with everyone, offer learning extensions to those who are ready to move on. Ideas include • "Read the interview with the author, and write a summary that highlights the important ideas."

Lesson Extension *(continued)*	• "Summarize the interview, and write down any other questions you may have wanted to ask the author."
	• "Summarize the interview, and write a letter to the author with any additional questions you may have."
Assessment	• In students' work, look for the organization of the summary, how they stretched their jottings, whether they use a topic sentence, whether they have a short overview of the text, and the structure of the finished product. This will guide your teaching and help you assess student understanding.

Planning Project-Based Learning

Project-based learning is a proven way to place performance tasks within a meaningful context and elicit the highest student engagement and understanding. "In a project-based approach, students work over an extended time period for a purpose beyond satisfying a school requirement—to build something, to create something, to respond

> **Project-based learning gives students real reasons to use their language skills**
>
> see Section 2, page 16

to a question they have, to solve a real problem, or to address an area of need" (Duke 2014). This type of learning also supports differentiation.

Megan's third graders are learning about the state of Michigan. She's identified the social studies and literacy standards she wants to meet and translated those standards into learning targets and performance tasks for her students (see Figure 3–9), who are free to choose a person to research based on their interests. Because Caleb and his family are music enthusiasts, he wants to research a famous musician from Michigan. He visits the Motown Museum in Detroit and decides to do his presentation on—and as—Ray Charles (see Figure 3–10). His presentation emphasizes what Ray Charles accomplished despite his personal challenges. In addition to meeting the identified standards, Caleb has learned that an individual can transcend personal difficulty—in this case, the challenges of racism and blindness—to become an important symbol and artistic voice.

Figure 3–9 From Standards to a Project-Based Learning Unit

Standard	Example Learning Target
CCSS.ELA-LITERACY.RI.3.2 Determine the main idea of a text; recount the key details and explain how they support the main idea.	• I can determine the main idea with supporting details.
CCSS.ELA-LITERACY.RI.3.4 Determine the meaning of general academic and domain-specific words and phrases in a text relevant to a grade 3 topic or subject area.	• I can understand new vocabulary through context of text.
CCSS.ELA-LITERACY.RI.3.7 Use information gained from illustrations (e.g., maps, photographs) and the words in a text to demonstrate understanding of the text (e.g., where, when, why, and how key events occur).	• I can reference images in my text to better understand my topic.
CCSS.ELA-LITERACY.RI.3.9 Compare and contrast the most important points and key details presented in two texts on the same topic.	• I can compare and contrast two or more texts to further my understanding.

Performance Task	Project-Based Learning Unit Description
• Student performs research, reading, and taking notes on a variety of sources, including Internet searches and personal interviews.	Students will choose to research a person from Michigan who has contributed to society. Students will choose how to teach an audience about this person. Students will be prepared to answer questions. Students will use a variety of resources in their research. The teacher teaches lessons to support the learning targets and progress on the project.

A template for planning a project-based learning unit is provided in Appendix A.

Figure 3–10 Caleb as Ray Charles

Even when everyone is studying the same topic, teachers can differentiate by collecting a wide range of resources. For this unit, Megan collected texts from the school library, Internet sites, and pamphlets from the Michigan Chamber of Commerce. She not only addressed the wide variety of reading levels in her classroom but also helped her students understand the wisdom of consulting a variety of sources when reading for information.

Project-based learning fosters differentiation because it allows students the space to outgrow what we or they think is possible. In our grade 4 and 5 multiage classroom, students began a unit on the history of our town, with the aim of sharing their learning in a display at the town hall. In small groups, they studied newspaper clippings, old maps, and property deeds. They visited some local landmarks and were especially taken with the Drayton Plains Nature Center, which they volunteered to help clean up. They also decided the center should have an outdoor classroom. They researched what materials and infrastructure were required, interviewed town managers and center personnel, and drafted and revised a plan with community input. Student teams raised money, chose and ordered tables (not only learning about durability, color, and style but also deciding to buy one that complied with the American with Disabilities Act), and designed concrete platforms (which included calculating the outdoor space's slope). The completed classroom is shown in Figure 3–11.

These students' research into town history made them aware of the legacies left by prior citizens, moved them to help maintain those legacies, and inspired them to contribute their own. They achieved so much more than meeting individual learning targets, because choice, interest, and teacher support ensured success. The local newspaper picked up this story, and the children and their teachers received an award from the "Keep Michigan Beautiful" organization. They now have a sense of how they can use their learning to make the world a better place.

Figure 3–11 Outdoor Classroom

When and How to Use Whole-Group Instruction

In Section 2, Debra cautioned about excessive use of whole-group instruction, but, as she noted, effective teachers use some whole-group instruction, and whole-group instruction can also play an important role in creating class community. Also, whole-group, student-led discussions can spark the engagement we want all our students to experience; they are appropriate when we are building common knowledge or experiences, such as after listening to a particular book read aloud or watching a video related to a content unit. Whole-group instruction is also efficient when many students have a common instructional need. Students who aren't necessarily the first with their hand in the air to answer a question are often those with the most creative insights to share; whole-group instruction opens doors for them to do so. In whole-group settings, students build energy and excitement about class goals, initiate class investigations of larger school and community issues, and suggest possible solutions to these issues.

With her kindergartners, Tara is using a whole-group interactive writing activity to focus on the learning target *understand that we choose the form of writing that best fits our purpose (reason)*. Prior to a class field trip to the zoo, the zookeeper visited the classroom and explained her job. After reviewing how much they had learned during the visit, the students were eager to thank her for her time and wisdom. Tara is aware that some students are more comfortable with reading and writing in front of the class than others. She calls on Aleecia to begin the letter for the class.

"*Dear* is a common way to start a letter. It helps communicate respect and affection, so let's start our letter with that. Aleecia, what does the word *Dear* start with?" Aleecia recently learned how to identify and write the initial capital consonant *D*, and doing so in front of her classmates is an important affirmation. As Aleecia returns to her seat, Tara asks Alex whether he thinks he can complete the word.

From her specific learning target assessments, she knows Alex is already reading and knows a lot of words by sight. After Alex has completed the word, the students complete the letter, with Tara acting as scribe but not including punctuation.

Next, Tara turns to Katia, who has recently been asking about punctuation, and together they helped the students decide where to put the commas and periods. Vince argues that an exclamation point should be used at the end of the final sentence—he wants to show that the class really appreciated the zookeeper's visit—and a spontaneous discussion about when it's appropriate to use an exclamation point emerges.

As part of her planning, Tara has identified a few students and skills to focus on as part of the class's interactive writing of the thank-you letter, but unplanned-for specifics such as the exclamation-point discussion also come up—a learning bonus. During the activity Tara notices that some students are still confused about comma use even after her clarifications, so she makes a note to revisit this topic in group instruction and individual conferences.

We won't cover every student's needs in a whole-group lesson or activity, but we can plan to hit some key learning targets, connect those targets to the learning trajectory of specific students, and then use the information we gather to plan further differentiation.

The whole-group aspects of a reading workshop reveal a poster-size portrait of the class as a whole, along with some snapshots of individual students. Whole-group instruction follows a predictable pattern, or rhythm: connection, demonstration/teaching, guided practice, recap, independent practice, sharing, lesson closure. This rhythm leads to the gradual release of responsibility (see Figure 3–12). Teacher moves are deliberate: explicit instruction, guided learning in teacher-student interaction, and finally a step toward independence. This pattern can play out in any order, as long as each element exists in every lesson.

Figure 3–12   Gradual Release of Responsibility

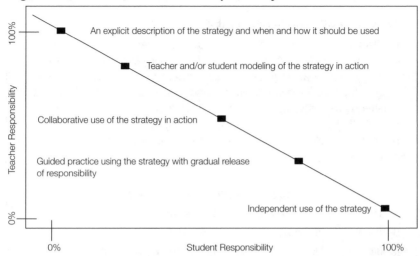

Adapted from Pearson and Gallagher 1983

When and How to Use Small-Group Instruction

As Debra discussed in Section 2, teachers use small-group instruction when they find, based on formative assessment, that a few students have similar needs. Small-group instruction extends the learning target, reaches beyond, and offers additional scaffolding. Students benefit from peer support, peer mentoring, and feeling part of a team as they work toward goals together.

Word study is an essential part of reading instruction that is often addressed in small-group work. Letter–sound and word knowledge varies greatly from student to student, so differentiation is key. In order to determine student strengths and needs, we administer a spelling inventory, such as the one in Figure 3–13. (For a detailed explanation of how to administer and use spelling inventories, see *Words Their Way*.) We then use this information to form word study groups. For example, if four of our students need to work on digraphs, we present this instruction to them as a group.

Figure 3–13a *Words Their Way* Elementary Spelling Inventory

Elementary Spelling Inventory (ESI)

The Elementary Spelling Inventory (ESI) covers more stages than the Primary Spelling Inventory (PSI). It can be used as early as first grade, particularly if a school system wants to use the same inventory across the elementary grades. The twenty-five words are ordered by difficulty to sample features of the letter name–alphabetic to derivational relations stages. Call out enough words so that you have at least five or six misspelled words to analyze. If any students spell more than twenty words correctly, use the Upper Level Spelling Inventory.

1. bed	I hopped out of bed this morning.	*bed*
2. ship	The ship sailed around the island.	*ship*
3. when	When will you come back?	*when*
4. lump	He had a lump on his head after he fell.	*lump*
5. float	I can float on the water with my new raft.	*float*
6. train	I rode the train to the next town.	*train*
7. place	I found a new place to put my books.	*place*
8. drive	I learned to drive a car.	*drive*
9. bright	The light is very bright.	*bright*
10. shopping	She went shopping for new shoes.	*shopping*
11. spoil	The food will spoil if it is not kept cool.	*spoil*
12. serving	The restaurant is serving dinner tonight.	*serving*
13. chewed	The dog chewed up my favorite sweater yesterday.	*chewed*
14. carries	She carries apples in her basket.	*carries*
15. marched	We marched in the parade.	*marched*
16. shower	The shower in the bathroom was very hot.	*shower*
17. bottle	The bottle broke into pieces on the tile floor.	*bottle*
18. favor	He did his brother a favor by taking out the trash.	*favor*
19. ripen	The fruit will ripen over the next few days.	*ripen*
20. cellar	I went down to the cellar for the can of paint.	*cellar*
21. pleasure	It was a pleasure to listen to the choir sing.	*pleasure*
22. fortunate	It was fortunate that the driver had snow tires.	*fortunate*
23. confident	I am confident that we can win the game.	*confident*
24. civilize	They wanted to civilize the forest people.	*civilize*
25. opposition	The coach said the opposition would be tough.	*opposition*

Figure 3–13b Words Their Way Elementary Spelling Inventory Feature Guide

Words Their Way Elementary Spelling Inventory Feature Guide

Student's Name: _Jake Fisher_ Teacher: _T. Atkinson_ Grade: _5_ Date: _September_

Words Spelled Correctly: _9 / 25_ Feature Points: _43 / 62_ Total: _52 / 87_

Spelling Stage: _Late Within Word Pattern_

SPELLING STAGES → Features →	EMERGENT LATE EARLY MIDDLE — Consonants Initial	Consonants Final	LETTER NAME-ALPHABETIC LATE EARLY MIDDLE — Short Vowels	Digraphs	Blends	WITHIN WORD PATTERN LATE EARLY MIDDLE — Long Vowels	Other Vowels	Inflected Endings	SYLLABLES AND AFFIXES LATE EARLY MIDDLE — Syllable Junctures	Unaccented Final Syllables	Harder Suffixes	OBSERVATIONAL RELATIONS — Bases or Roots	Feature Points	Words Spelled Correctly
1. bed	b✓	d✓	e✓										3	1
2. ship		p✓	i✓	sh✓									3	1
3. when			e✓	wh✓									2	1
4. lump	l✓		u✓		mp✓								3	1
5. float		t✓			fl✓	oa✓							3	1
6. train		n✓			tr✓	ai✓							3	1
7. place					pl✓	a-e✓							2	1
8. drive		v✓			dr✓	i-e✓							3	1
9. bright					br✓	Igh i-e✓							1	
10. shopping			o✓	sh✓				pping					2	
11. spoil					sp✓		oi oy						1	1
12. serving							er✓	ving✓					2	
13. chewed				ch✓			ee oo	ed✓					2	
14. carries							ar✓	ies	rr				1	
15. marched				ch✓			ar✓	ed✓					3	
16. shower				sh✓			ow✓			er✓			3	
17. bottle									tt✓	le			1	
18. favor									v✓	or			1	
19. ripen									p	en				
20. cellar									ll	ar✓			1	
21. pleasure											ure	pleas✓	1	1
22. fortunate							or✓				ate✓	fortun	2	
23. confident											ent	confid		
24. civilize											ize	civil		
25. opposition											tion	pos		
Totals	7 / 7		5 / 5	6 / 6	7 / 7	4 / 5	5 / 7	3 / 5	2 / 5	2 / 5	1 / 5	1 / 5	43	9

Bear, Donald R.; Invernizzi, Marcia A.; Templeton, Shane; Johnston, Francine A., _Words Their Way: Word Study for Phonics, Vocabulary, and Spelling Instruction_, 6th ed. © 2016, p. 324. Reprinted by permission of Pearson Education, Inc., New York, New York.

Differentiated Reading Instruction in Your Classroom **55**

Launching her first reading unit in grade 1, Elissa teaches a lesson on how readers form good habits. In collaboration with her students, she creates a chart headed "What We Know About Print." Based on the results of a Developmental Reading Assessment pretest, Elissa follows up her lesson with small-group work on, depending upon the group, directionality, one-to-one matching, auditory memory, sound/symbol connection, and high-frequency words. Small-group instruction like this is goal-driven and intentional, and supportive feedback steers students toward independence.

Figure 3–14 shows the small-group instruction plan for Elissa's classroom, including the days the groups are to meet and the area of focus. Groups needing the most support meet with Elissa daily, at least initially. Groups reading more independently may meet with her less frequently. Once Elissa has gotten to know her students through observation, conferences, and formative assessment, she changes the group makeup frequently based on identified needs.

Figure 3–14 Small-Group Instructional Plan

Reading Groups			
Group 1	TJ (1) Jacob (1)	Focus: beginning letters/sounds high-frequency words	M–F
Group 2	Lucas (1) Mikey (1) Nick (2)	Focus: letters/sounds high-frequency words	M–F
Group 3	Wyatt (3) Alexis (3)	Focus: spelling/writing high-frequency words quickly	M–F

Group 4	Taggert (6)	Focus:	M, W, F
	Zoey M. (6)	decoding words using strategies	
	Lee (6)	self-correcting	
		fluency	
Group 5	Bailey (6)	Focus:	M, W
	Brianna (6)	decoding words using strategies	
	Reagan (6)	retelling with details	
Group 6	Austin (8)	Focus:	T, TH
	Evan (8)	self-correcting	
	Becky (8)		
Group 7	Maddie (8)	Focus:	T, TH
	Lannie (8)	adding details to retelling	
	Taylen (10)		
Group 8	Fatima (16)	Focus: retelling longer texts with details	W, F
	Isla (16)		
	Zoey (16)		
Group 9	Audrey (18)	Focus:	W, F
	Riley (18)	Talking and writing about books	
	Marcus (24)		

When and How to Use Independent Work Time

When students are working independently they are engaged in a productive struggle: Can they transfer their whole-group learning to a different context on their own? The question requires more than a yes or no answer, since these new contexts add new layers of complexity and understanding. Students are focused on becoming self-directed and accountable for their own learning. Working independently lets teacher and student know what the student can hold on to from the day's learning. While students are working, we meet with several of them but not all. Therefore it's essential that students document their learning in some way. And all students know that when the work session ends, a whole-group sharing session will help clarify some aspect of their learning based on what we have observed.

Sticky notes displaying icons (see Figure 3–15) are one way students document their independent and small-group work. These symbols help us quickly assess student understanding, and we can then use the information during our conferences with students. If a partnership or individual has used the confusing symbol, we find out what hasn't been understood. An LOL accompanied by laughter clues us in to a sense of humor.

Figure 3–15   Reading-Response Sticky Note Icons

Conferring

A conference is an excellent follow-up to any form of assessment. Patrick Allen (2009) says:

> Conferring is the keystone of my readers' workshop. I find that when I sit down with a reader, I'm better able to get a handle on his/her emerging understandings and thinking than I am when I work with a small group. I love the shoulder-to shoulder, eye-to-eye commitment we make to one another during each and every conference. There's something special about making discoveries, hashing out thinking, wondering [together]. (33)

Conferences usually take place while the students are reading independently but sometimes during partner/small-group work. We may plan a conference with a specific student to provide targeted instruction based on earlier assessment or decide to have one on the spot. If we have a specific skill in mind, we teach it, but if the conference is an on-the-spot assessment and goal setting, we investigate what the student is doing well and might do next to grow, compliment what the student is doing well, and then teach what the student can try next. We make the investigation a conversation in which we prompt the student to reflect on his or her learning.

Reading conferences typically last about five minutes. By conferring with four or five students every day, we can meet with twenty to twenty-five students each week; each and every student receives regular, individually targeted instruction. Some teachers wear a special necklace or hat when they are conducting conferences to signal that they may be interrupted only for emergencies. We move from child to child rather than have the children come to us, to minimize disruptions. Speaking just above a whisper lets nearby students overhear and use the ideas being discussed.

Nichole wanted her fifth graders to gain insight into the characters in *Edward's Eyes* (2009), by Patricia MacLachlan, a story she was going to read aloud. Her key learning targets were to help the students (1) build theories about the characters and gather evidence to support their ideas; (2) move from inference to interpretation; and (3) compare characters within, between, and among texts. Planning her instruction, she made a large anchor chart for display, as well as individual versions students could keep in their reading notebook.

After reading the story, Nichole explained that readers not only step inside the story and get lost in it but also pull back, step outside the story, and try to understand and empathize with the characters. She then asked students to record their thinking about a character of their choice on a chart (see Figure 3–16) and develop these ideas during a conversation with their partner. She assessed these partner conversations using the checklist in Figure 3–17. Nichole also did some teaching as part of her assessment, but she was primarily gathering information on which to plan future teaching regarding these learning targets.

Figure 3–16 Developing Theories About a Character

I already think that . . .	I wonder why . . . Maybe it is because . . .	I can't believe that . . . Maybe now I think . . .

Figure 3–17 Reflection Form for Understanding and Empathizing with a Character

Reflection Form for Understanding and Empathizing with a Character	
Student Name:	
Developing Theories About Characters	
Steps outside the story to develop ideas about the characters.	
Notices a character's actions and how other characters treat the character.	
Notices when characters act in surprising ways.	
Thinks about the importance of objects to the characters.	
Uses precise, exact words to describe the characters.	
From Inference Toward Interpretation	
Searches for patterns and keeps theories in mind.	
Notices characters' motivations and struggles.	

(continues)

Figure 3–17 *(continued)*

From Inference Toward Interpretation *(continued)*	
Builds complex theories about characters using prompts.	
Notices recurring themes and details.	
Comparing Characters	
Compares characters and situations.	
Compares how characters face and overcome challenges.	
Compares how characters play parallel roles.	
Pushes self and others to make deeper comparisons among characters.	
Reflecting on Stories and Ourselves	
Uses motifs to spark lasting thoughts.	
Analyzes strengths and ways to grow.	

During her conferring time, Nichole uses this reflection form to guide her conversation with a student. The form provides the student with the spectrum of skills within his grasp, if not today, in the not-too-distant future, and gives both the teacher and student language to name his strengths and what's worth reaching for.

Setting Individual Learning Goals

Some conferences focus on helping students set their own learning goals. Unlike a learning target, which is initiated for the whole group, goals are personal and help a child reach beyond what she or he can already do. While the learning goals are personal, the celebration of achievement is not. In our school, students celebrate their growth by inviting their families to a special lunch where they share their goals and the progress they've noted in their data notebooks.

Kimberly begins setting shared goals with her kindergartners in the fall. She gives a pretest to determine each child's ability to identify lowercase letters and letter sounds and uses this information to create small instructional groups. As the year proceeds, she records students' progress using different-color highlighters. Children keep these forms in a notebook and are able to monitor their progress and celebrate their achievement.

Planning Intervention

As thoughtful as we are in planning instruction, not all learning will happen as we hope. That's to be expected. We cannot assume all students will achieve a learning target on a certain day and time; human learning cannot be programmed. Our goal is to get all the students in our classroom as close as we can to meeting or exceeding certain standards. Some students will learn faster than we anticipated; some will require additional time and support. That doesn't mean we lower our expectations of what children can do; rather, we increase our support. We teach responsively. When we see student readers struggle, we "increase the amount of reading instruction offered" and "are far more likely to see the growth needed to catch up" (Allington 2009).

> **Schools that hold data meetings based on formative assessment of students in need of intervention find success**
>
> see Section 2, page 19

Reading interventions must be provided by knowledgeable teachers. At our school, we hold a two-hour grade-level literacy team meeting each quarter. The reading interventionist, speech and language pathologist, special education teacher, ELL teacher, and I evaluate each struggling reader. We then create an intervention plan that ensures all instruction is aligned (see the example in Figure 3–18). We start with what we know about the student's strengths; then we identify the logical next steps that will support the student, fill in the gaps, and guide him or her toward independence. The goal is short lived and attainable. If the student does not demonstrate growth within four or five weeks, we meet again and design a new plan.

Every intervention plan includes the gradual release of responsibility as an essential strategy to support student independence. We also create a slope graph that demonstrates growth visually. It's important that the student be able to notice progress and realize that her or his identity as uncertain or struggling is not fixed. With the right support, struggle need be only temporary.

Supporting Growth Beyond Our Expectations

Our goal is for our students to achieve more than we can imagine, so we introduce above-grade-level learning targets when students demonstrate they are ready for them. Student choice is a key component to stretching each student to his or her full potential. The choices we offer include:

- More complex texts, so they can increase their level of comprehension.
- Immersive content (student-initiated projects or author studies, for example), so they can explore new ideas triggered by their own curiosity.
- Book clubs, so they can push one another's thinking to new levels.

Students who are not consistently pushed to their capacity begin to underperform. There is so much potential in each child in our classroom. Some we see hints of; some is hidden. Without providing every student the opportunity to exceed what she or he can do in the present moment, we risk leaving that potential unrealized. Oh, the joy we feel when our students achieve more than they thought possible!

Figure 3–18. Intervention Plan

Intervention Plan for:	**Date:** 11/5/12
Teacher: Kras	**Expected Duration:** 2 weeks
Start Date: 11/5/12 **End Date:** 11/19/12	
Strengths: Can write name; can identify some letters; knows some sounds; comments on pictures in books	

Specific Goal: Student will be able to identify, write, and provide a sound for letters: *p, b, m, t, d, n*

How and when will you assess the goal? What will you use in between to monitor progress?

Daily assessment by review, reading, word study, and writing

What will you teach? Be specific

Interventionist

Today I am going to teach you about the letter **p**.

All letters make a sound and **p** says \p\

Your lips are together, air bursts out of your lips, your motor is off

I put my fist by my shoulder and spring my fingers open to help my mouth remember

Make the sound \p\.

This is the letter **p**. (*Show magnetic letter*)

Trace the letter **p** with your finger like this, (*Model*) and say "**p**."

This is how you write the letter **p**. (*Model*) Now, you try it a few times.

How will you teach it?

Teacher and Speech–Language Pathologist:

5 times per week in a small group

Daily writing and word stretching

Daily reading of perfectly matched books

How will the plan be communicated to and supported by the parent?

Plan will be shared with the student and family

In Section 1, I cited a recent article that dismissed differentiation as too hard. I hope that you now feel confident in your belief that differentiated reading instruction is not only worthy but achievable in your classroom. Through the tools you've gained from this section —observation; formative assessment; whole-group, small-group, and individual work time; workshop structure; project-based learning; goal-setting and intervention plans—you can see more students learn more in your classroom. I hope you can imagine how you might try one piece of this work, but I'm even more eager for you to see what can happen when you use these tools together. Too often in teaching today, teachers don't feel the joy of the work but instead are disengaged by the burden of expectations and their uncertainty of how to meet those expectations. You can do this work; you just needed to know how. I've seen many teachers find new joy in their teaching through differentiation because it is effective. I know you can, too.

AFTERWORD

NELL K. DUKE

By this point, you have a wealth of knowledge about how to carry out differentiated reading instruction. For example, you have learned how to distribute instructional time in whole-class versus small-group configurations. You have learned how to provide students with multiple opportunities to write and talk about what they read each day. You have learned how to approach the design of lessons that respond to students, not just standards. You have learned to use project-based learning to engage students in meaningful pursuit and communication of information and ideas. I thought we'd close this book by stepping back from the *how to* and returning to the *why to*, a matter Lynn and Debra took up in Sections 1 and 2 and that was likely on your mind from the moment you decided to read this book. Most fundamentally, we differentiate reading instruction because every child deserves the opportunity to become a purposeful and effective reader.

1. Every child *deserves* to read texts on topics of personal interest and texts by authors she or he admires.
2. Every child *deserves* to develop deep expertise on specific topics and to be acknowledged for that expertise.
3. Every child *deserves* to read and write daily for purposes beyond practice, routine, or "doing school."
4. Every child *deserves* to know that there are high expectations for his or her thinking and learning.
5. Every child *deserves* to participate in setting personal learning goals.

6. Every child *deserves* the support necessary to be able to engage productively with classroom work.
7. Every child *deserves* instruction that is targeted to his or her strengths and needs.

I thank Lynn and Debra for their unrelenting efforts to provide children with the reading instruction they deserve, and I thank you for joining in this work.

APPENDIX A

Ways to share thinking about a book in writing:

- *Thinking notebooks.* Children record in a notebook strategies they use, emphasizing how the strategy helped them understand or what it prompted them to think about.
- *Post-it notes* to highlight strategies being used in a text.
- *Double-entry (two-column) journals* about the reading process and reading strategies. For example, students may copy a quotation from a text in the first column and record their thinking about the quotation in the second.
- *Fluency responses.* Children write down everything they think about a short text or excerpt.
- *Stop and jot.* Stop reading aloud at predetermined places, and have children write down their interpretation of what is happening.
- *Venn diagrams* showing inferences in the intersecting section and the source of the inferences in the outlying circles.
- *Column charts* (three or more columns) in which students can compare their thinking over the course of several readings of a text or an excerpt.
- *Letters* to other readers and authors about one's thinking/use of a strategy.
- *Highlighting* a particular kind of thinking or strategy.
- *Story maps/webs* capturing children's thinking about important themes or topics.

Artistic ways to share thinking about a book:

- Sketching images and other manifestations of thinking during reading.
- Group depictions of text concepts and use of strategies during reading.
- Artistic metaphors—creating a visual metaphor for thinking during reading.
- Artistic timelines to show changes in thinking over time.
- Photographs of the mind—quick images from particular moments in a text.

Ways to share thinking about a book orally:

- *Think-pair-share.* A collaborative strategy in which students work together on a task or question. First, students consider the prompt on their own, then share and push their thinking further with a classmate.
- *3-2-1 Bridge.* In this strategy, students build bridges between prior knowledge and new knowledge gained from a text. What are the 3—thoughts—2—ideas—and—1—analogy—that they can create about the topic before and then after reading the text? (Adapted from Ritchhart 2011)
- *See, Think, Wonder.* This strategy helps students observe and interpret by giving them specific questions to answer: What do you *see*? What do you *think* about that? What does it make you *wonder*? (Adapted from Ritchhart 2011)
- *Compass points.* Students discuss their comprehension of a text by identifying directional points that represent E = excited, W = worrisome, N = need to know, and S = suggestions to move forward or to identify the current stance. (Adapted from Ritchhart 2011)

- *Question sorts.* Students identify and then group questions into similar groups. Why? How would it be different if? What are the reasons? What would change if? What is the purpose?
- *Book clubs and literature circles.* Students apply reading strategies and specific discussion techniques to collaborate on meaning-making of texts.
- *Strategy study groups.* Groups that share new uses they have found for strategies or how use of a strategy is different in a new genre.

APPENDIX B

Project-Based Unit-Planning Template

Project Name: Number of Sessions:

Project Developer(s):

Project/Students' Purpose: Audience: Final Product:

Focal Genre(s): Domain(s): Key Standards:

Project Launch	Text	Whole-Class Lesson	Small-Group, Partner, and Individual Work	Whole-Class Wrap-Up	Standards Addressed
(Session 1)					

Reading and Research Phase*	Text	Whole-Class Lesson	Small-Group, Partner, and Individual Work	Whole-Class Wrap-Up	Standards Addressed
Session 2					
Session 3					
Session 4					
Session 5 (add sessions as needed)					

(continues)

Writing and Research Phase*	Text	Whole-Class Lesson	Small-Group, Partner, and Individual Work	Whole-Class Wrap-Up	Standards Addressed
Session 6					
Session 7					
Session 8					
Session 9					
Session 10 (add sessions as needed)					

Revision and Editing Phase	Text	Whole-Class Lesson	Small-Group, Partner, and Individual Work	Whole-Class Wrap-Up	Standards Addressed
Session 11					
Session 12					
Session 13					
Session 14					
Session 15 (add sessions as needed)					

**Presentation
and Celebration**

*A reminder that the phases are not rigid. Some writing will occur during Reading and Research, and some reading will occur during Writing and Research.

From Nell Duke, *Inside Information: Developing Powerful Readers and Writers of Informational Text Through Project-Based Instruction* (2014).

A Microsoft Word version of this document is posted at http://umich.edu/~nkduke/ so you can add lessons/sessions and change the form as needed.

REFERENCES

Allen, P. 2009. *Conferring: The Keystone of Reader's Workshop*. Portland, ME: Stenhouse.

Allington, R. 2009. *What Really Matters in Response to Intervention: Research-Based Designs*. Boston: Allyn and Bacon.

Allington, R. L., and P. H. Johnston. 2002. *Reading to Learn: Lessons from Exemplary Fourth-Grade Classrooms*. New York: Guilford.

Au, K. 2005. *Multicultural Issues and Literacy Achievement*. Mahwah, NJ: Erlbaum.

August, D., and T. Shanahan, eds. 2006. *Developing Literacy in Second-Language Learners: Report of the National Literacy Panel on Language Minority Children and Youth*. Mahwah, NJ: Erlbaum.

Barnes, D. 1976. *From Communication to Curriculum*. Harmondsworth, UK: Penguin.

Barr, R., and R. Dreeben. 1991. "Grouping Students for Reading Instruction." In *Handbook of Reading Research*, vol. 2, edited by R. Barr, M. L. Kamil, P. B. Mosenthal, and P. D. Pearson, 885–910. New York: Longman.

Barron, B., and L. Darling-Hammond. 2008. *Teaching for Meaningful Learning: A Review of Research on Inquiry-Based and Cooperative Learning*. San Francisco, CA: Jossey-Bass.

Beck, I., and M. McKeown. 2007. "Increasing Young Low-Income Children's Oral Vocabulary Repertoires Through Rich and Focused Instruction." *Elementary School Journal* 107 (3): 251–71.

Bohn, C. M., A. D. Roehrig, and M. Pressley. 2004. "The First Days of School in the Classrooms of Two More Effective and Four Less Effective Primary-Grade Teachers." *The Elementary School Journal* 104: 271–87.

Chinn, C., R. C. Anderson, and M. Waggoner, M. 2001. "Patterns of Discourse During Two Kinds of Literature Discussion." *Reading Research Quarterly* 36 (4): 378–411.

Chorzempa, B. F., and S. Graham. 2006. "Primary-Grade Teachers' Use of Within-Class Ability Grouping in Reading." *Journal of Educational Psychology* 98: 529–41.

Connor, C., F. Morrison, B. Fishman, S. Giuliani, M. Luck, P. Underwood, A. Bayraktar, E. Crowe, and C. Schatschneider. 2011. "Testing the Impact of Child Characteristics × Instruction Interactions on Third Graders' Reading Comprehension by Differentiating Literacy Instruction." *Reading Research Quarterly* 46 (3): 189–221.

Daniels, H. 2002. *Literature Circles: Voice and Choice in Book Clubs and Reading Groups*, 2nd ed. Portland, ME: Stenhouse.

Dillard, Annie. 2103. *The Writing Life*. New York: Harper Perennial.

Duke, N. K. 2014. *Inside Information: Developing Powerful Readers and Writers of Informational Text Through Project-Based Instruction*. New York: Scholastic.

Ehri, L., S. Nunes, D. Willows, B. Schuster, Z. Yaghoub-Zadeh, and T. Shanahan. 2001. "Phonemic Awareness Instruction Helps Children Learn to Read: Evidence from the National Reading Panel's Meta-Analysis." *Reading Research Quarterly* 36 (3): 250–87.

Elbaum, B., S. Vaughn, M. T. Hughes, S. W. Moody, and J. S. Schumm. 2000. "A Meta-Analytic Review of the Effect of Instructional Grouping Format on the Reading Outcomes of Students with Disabilities." In *Issues* and Research in Special Education, edited by R. Gersten, E. Schiller, J. S. Schumm, and S. Vaughn, 105–35. Hillsdale, NJ: Erlbaum.

Foorman, B. R., and J. Torgesen. 2001. "Critical Elements of Classroom and Small-Group Instruction Promote Reading Success in All Children." *Learning Disabilities Research and Practice* 16: 203–12.

Fuchs, D., L. S. Fuchs, P. G. Mathes, and D. C. Simmons. 1997. "Peer-Assisted Learning Strategies: Making Classrooms More Responsive to Diversity." *American Educational Research Journal* 34: 174–206.

Fuchs, D., L. Fuchs, and S. Vaughn, eds. 2008. *Response to Intervention: A Framework for Reading Educators*. Newark, DE: International Reading Association.

Garas-York, K., L. E. Shanahan, and J. F. Almasi. 2013. "Comprehension: High-Level Talk and Writing About Texts." In *Handbook on Effective Literacy Instruction*, edited by B. M. Taylor and N. K. Duke, 246–78. New York: Guilford.

Glasswell, K. 2001. "The Matthew Effects in Writing: The Patterning of Differences in Classrooms K–7." *Reading Research Quarterly* 36 (4): 348–49.

Goatley, V., C. Brock, and T. Raphael. 1995. "Diverse Learners Participating in Regular Education 'Book Clubs.'" *Reading Research Quarterly* 30: 352–80.

Graves, A. W., R. Gersten, and D. Haager. 2004. "Literacy Instruction in Multiple-Language First-Grade Classrooms: Linking Student Outcomes to Observed Instructional Practice." *Learning Disabilities Research & Practice* 19: 262–72.

Gunn, B., K. Smolkowski, A. Biglan, C. Black, and J. Blair. 2005. "Fostering the Development of Reading Skills Through Supplemental Instruction: Results for Hispanic and Non-Hispanic Students." *Journal of Special Education* 39: 66–85.

Guthrie, J., A. McRae, D. Coddington, S. Klauda, A. Wigfield, and P. Barbosa. 2009. "Impacts of Comprehensive Reading Instruction on Diverse Outcomes of Low-Achieving and High-Achieving Readers." *Journal of Learning Disabilities* 42: 195–214.

Guthrie, J. T., A. McRae, and S. Klauda. 2007. "Contributions of Concept-Oriented Reading Instruction to Knowledge About Interventions for Motivation in Reading." *Educational Psychologist* 43: 237–50.

Guthrie, J. T., A. Wigfield, P. Barbosa, K. C. Perencevich, A. Taboada, M. H. Davis, et al. 2004. "Increasing Reading Comprehension and Engagement Through Concept-Oriented Reading Instruction." *Journal of Educational Psychology* 96: 403–23.

Halvorsen, A., N. K. Duke, K. A. Brugar, M. K. Block, S. L. Strachan, M. B. Berka, and J. M. Brown. 2014. "Narrowing the Achievement Gap in Second-Grade Social Studies and Content Area Literacy: The Promise of a Project-Based Approach." *Theory and Research in Social Education* 40: 198–229.

Hart, B., and T. R. Risley. 2003. "The Early Catastrophe: The 30 Million Word Gap by Age 4." *American Educator* 27 (1): 4–9.

Hattie, J. 2009. *Visible Learning: A Synthesis of over 800 Meta-Analyses Relating to Achievement*. New York: Routledge.

Hattie, J., and H. Timperley. 2007. "The Power of Feedback." *Review of Educational Research* 77: 81–112.

Helman, L., ed. 2009. *Literacy Development with English Learners: Research-Based Instruction in Grades K–6*. New York: Guilford Press.

Heritage, M. 2013. *Formative Assessment in Practice: A Process of Inquiry and Action*. Cambridge, MA: Harvard Education Press.

Heritage, M., J. Kim, T. Vendlinski, and J. Herman. 2009. "From Evidence to Action: A Seamless Process in Formative Assessment." *Educational Measurement: Issues and Practices* 28: 24–31.

Hiebert, E. H., and B. M. Taylor. 1998. "Beginning Reading Instruction: Research on Early Interventions." In *Handbook of Reading Research*, vol. 3, edited by M. L. Kamil, P. B. Mosenthal, P. D. Pearson, and R. Barr, 455–82. Mahwah, NJ: Lawrence Erlbaum.

Johnson, D. W., and R. T. Johnson. 2009. "An Educational Psychology Success Story: Social Interdependence Theory and Cooperative Learning." *Educational Researcher* 38 (5): 365–79.

Keene, E. O., and S. Zimmermann. 2007. *Mosaic of Thought: The Power of Comprehention Strategy Instruction*, 2nd ed. Portsmouth, NH: Heinemann.

Kuhn, M., P. Schwanenflugel, and E. Meisinger. 2010. "Aligning Theory and Assessment of Reading Fluency: Automaticity, Prosody, and Definitions of Fluency." *Reading Research Quarterly* 45 (2): 230–51.

Kuhn, M., and S. Stahl. 2003. "Fluency: A Review of Developmental and Remedial Practices." *Journal of Educational Psychology* 95 (1): 3–21.

Lapp, D., D. Fisher, and T. D. Wolsey. 2009. *Literacy Growth for Every Child: Differentiated Small-Group Instruction, K–6*. New York: Guilford.

Lee, O., C. Buxton, S. Lewis, and K. LeRoy. 2006. "Science Inquiry and Student Diversity: Enhanced Abilities and Continuing Difficulties After an Instructional Intervention." *Science Teaching* 43 (7): 607–36.

Little, J. W., M. Gearhart, M. Curry, and J. Kafka. 2003. "Looking at Student Work for Teacher Learning, Teacher Community, and School Reform." *Phi Delta Kappan* 85 (3): 185–92.

MacLaughlin, Patricia. 2009. *Edward's Eyes*. New York: Atheneum Books for Young Readers.

Mathes, P. G., C. A. Denton, J. M. Fletcher, J. L. Anthony, D. J. Francis, and C. Schatschneider. 2005. "The Effects of Theoretically Different Instruction and Student Characteristics on the Skills of Struggling Readers." *Reading Research Quarterly* 40: 148–82.

Matsumura, L. C., G. Patthey-Chavez, R. Valdes, and H. Garnier. 2002. "Teacher Feedback, Writing Assignment Quality, and Third-Grade Students' Revision in Lower- and Higher-Achieving Urban Schools." *Elementary School Journal* 103: 3–25.

McCarthy, S. 1994. "Authors, Text, and Talk: The Internalization of Dialogue from Social Interaction During Writing." *Reading Research Quarterly* 29: 200–31.

McIntyre, E., D. W. Kyle, and G. H. Moore. 2006. "A Primary-Grade Teacher's Guidance Toward Small-Group Dialogue." *Reading Research Quarterly* 41 (1): 36–66.

McIntyre, E., and J. D. Turner. 2013. "Culturally Responsive Literacy Instruction." In *Handbook on Effective Literacy Instruction*, edited by B. M. Taylor and N. K. Duke, 137–61. New York: Guilford.

Miller, D., and B. Moss. 2013. *No More Independent Reading Without Support.* Portsmouth, NH: Heinemann.

Moss, Connie, and Susan Brookhart. 2012. *Learning Targets: Helping Students Aim for Understanding in Today's Lesson.* Alexandria, VA: ASCD.

National Center for Educational Evaluation and Regional Assistance. 2014. "Teaching Academic Content and Literacy to English Learners in Elementary and Middle School." Accessed at http://ies.ed.gov/ncee/wwc/pdf/practice _guide/english_learners_pg_040114.pdf on August 8, 2014.

National Center for Educational Statistics. 2014. *Report of Eighth Grade NAEP Reading Results.* Accessed at nces.ed.gov/nationsreportcard/naepdata /report.aspx7app=NDE&p on August 8, 2014.

National Reading Panel. 2000. *The National Reading Panel Report.* Washington, DC: National Institute of Child Health and Human Development.

Palincsar, A., and A. Brown. 1986. "Reciprocal Teaching of Comprehension-Fostering and Comprehension-Monitoring Activities." *Cognition and Instruction* 2: 117–75.

Pearson, P. D., and M. C. Gallagher. 1983. "The Instruction of Reading Comprehension." *Contemporary Educational Psychology* 8: 317–44.

Peterson, D. S. 2013a. "Balanced, Differentiated Teaching: Explicit Instruction, Scaffolded Support, and Active Student Responding." In *Handbook on Effective Literacy Instruction*, edited by B. M. Taylor and N. K. Duke, 88–105. New York: Guilford.

Peterson, D. S. 2013b. "Professional Learning: Professional Learning Communities, Whole-School Meetings, and Cross-School Sharing." In *Handbook on Effective Literacy Instruction*, edited by B. M. Taylor and N. K. Duke, 530–54. New York: Guilford.

Peterson, D. S., and B. M. Taylor. 2012. "Using Higher-Order Questioning to Accelerate Students' Growth in Reading." *The Reading Teacher* 65 (5): 295–304.

Pressley, M. 2006. *Reading Instruction That Works: The Case for Balanced Teaching*, 3rd ed. New York: Guilford.

Pressley, M., S. E. Dolezal, L. M. Raphael, L. Mohan, A. D. Roehrig, and K. Bogner. 2003. *Motivating Primary-Grade Students*. New York: Guilford.

Pressley, M., L. Mohan, L. M. Raphael, and L. Fingeret. 2007. "How Does Bennett Woods Elementary School Produce Such High Reading and Writing Achievement?" *Journal of Educational Psychology* 99 (2): 221–40.

Purcell-Gates, V., N. K. Duke, and J. A. Martineau. 2007. "Learning to Read and Write Genre-Specific Text: Roles of Authentic Experience and Explicit Teaching." *Reading Research Quarterly* 42 (1): 8–45.

RAND Reading Study Group. 2002. *Reading for Understanding: Toward an R & D Program in Reading Comprehension*. Santa Monica, CA: RAND Corporation.

Reutzel, D. R., P. C. Fawson, and J. A. Smith. 2008. "Reconsidering Silent Sustained Reading: An Exploratory Study of Scaffolded Silent Reading." *Journal of Educational Research* 102 (1): 37–50.

Ritchhart, R., M. Church, and K. Morrison. 2011. *Making Thinking Visible: How to Promote Engagement, Understanding, and Independence for All Learners*. Hoboken, NJ: Jossey-Bass.

Roehrig, A. D., E. H. Brinkerhoff, E. S. Rawls, and T. Pressley. 2013. "Motivating Classroom Practices to Support Effective Literacy Instruction." In *Handbook on Effective Literacy Instruction*, edited by B. M. Taylor and N. K. Duke, 13–45. New York: Guilford.

Saunders, W. M., and C. Goldenberg. 1999. "Effects of Instructional Conversations and Literature Logs on Limited- and Fluent-English-Proficient Students' Story Comprehension and Thematic Understanding." *Elementary School Journal* 99 (4): 277–301.

Scanlon, D. M., L. M. Gelzheiser, F. R. Vellutino, C. Schatschneider, and J. M. Sweeney. 2008. "Reducing the Incidence of Early Reading Difficulties: Professional Development for Classroom Teachers Versus Direct Intervention for Children." *Learning and Individual Differences* 18 (3): 346–59.

Serravallo, J. 2010. *Teaching Reading in Small Groups: Differentiated Instruction for Building Strategic, Independent Readers*. Portsmouth, NH: Heinemann.

Snow, C. E., M. S. Burns, and P. Griffin. 1998. *Preventing Reading Difficulties in Young Children*. Washington, DC: National Academy Press.

Sotor, A. O., I. A. Wilkinson, P. K. Murphy, L. Lodge, K. Reninger, and M. Edwards. 2008. "What the Discourse Tells Us: Talk and Indicators of High-Level Comprehension." *International Journal of Educational Research* 48 (1): 740–64.

Taylor, B. M. 2011. *Catching Schools: An Action Guide to School-Wide Reading Improvement*. Portsmouth, NH: Heinemann.

———. 2013. "Grouping Practices, Independent Learning Activities, and Effective Instruction." In *Handbook on Effective Literacy Instruction*, edited by B. M. Taylor and N. K. Duke, 72–87. New York: Guilford.

Taylor, B. M., P. D. Pearson, K. Clark, and S. Walpole. 2000. "Effective Schools and Accomplished Teachers: Lessons About Primary Grade Reading Instruction in Low-Income Schools." *The Elementary School Journal* 101: 121–65.

Taylor, B. M., P. D. Pearson, D. S. Peterson, and M. C. Rodriguez. 2003. "Reading Growth in High-Poverty Classrooms: The Influence of Teacher Practices That Encourage Cognitive Engagement in Literacy Learning." *The Elementary School Journal* 104: 3–28.

———. 2005. "The CIERA School Change Framework: An Evidence-Based Approach to Professional Development and School Reading Improvement." *Reading Research Quarterly* 40 (1): 40–69.

Taylor, B. M., and D. S. Peterson. 2006. *The Impact of the School Change Framework in Twenty-Three Minnesota REA Schools*. St. Paul: University of Minnesota, Minnesota Center for Reading Research.

Taylor, B. M., D. S. Peterson, M. Marx, and M. Chein. 2007. "Scaling Up a Reading Reform." In *Effective Instruction for Struggling Readers K–6*, edited by B. M. Taylor and J. E. Ysseldyke, 216–34. New York: Teachers College Press.

Taylor, B. M., D. S. Peterson, P. D. Pearson, and M. C. Rodriguez. 2002. "Looking Inside Classrooms: Reflecting on the 'How' as Well as the 'What' in Effective Reading Instruction." *The Reading Teacher* 56: 70–79.

Teale, W. H., and L. B. Gambrell. 2007. "Raising Urban Students' Literacy Achievement by Engaging in Authentic, Challenging Work." *The Reading Teacher* 60 (8): 728–39.

Tyner, B. 2009. *Small-Group Reading Instruction: A Differentiated Teaching Model for Beginning and Struggling Readers.* Newark, DE: International Reading Association.

Tyner, B., and S. E. Green. 2005. *Small-Group Reading Instruction: A Differentiated Teaching Model for Intermediate Grade Readers, Grades 3–8.* Newark, DE: International Reading Association.

Valencia, S. W., and M. R. Riddle Buly. 2004. "What Struggling Readers REALLY Need." *The Reading Teacher* 57: 520–33.

Vaughn, S., P. Mathes, S. Linan-Thompson, P. Cirino, C. Carlson, S. Pollard-Durdola et al. 2006. "Effectiveness of an English Intervention for First-Grade English Language Learners at Risk for Reading Problems." *The Elementary School Journal* 107: 153–80.

Wieseman, K. C., and D. Cadwell. 2005. "Local History and Problem-Based Learning." *Social Studies and the Young Learner* 18 (1): 11–14.